Between visits to Italy, 1......... ......y found time to be a political reporter for *The Australian*, New York correspondent for *The Sydney Morning Herald*, Editor of *The Bulletin*, and a breakfast presenter for ABC radio. He is currently the anthropology writer for *The Sydney Morning Herald*, and contributes regularly on travel, food and popular culture to *The Age*, the ABC and *BRW* magazine. His nine books include *The 100 Things Everyone Needs to Know about Australia*, *Essential Places*—a book about ideas and where they started, and *The Obsessive Traveller, or Why I Don't Steal Towels From Great Hotels Any More*.

THE 100 THINGS EVERYONE NEEDS TO KNOW ABOUT ITALY

DAVID DALE

Illustrations by Cathy Wilcox

Pan Macmillan Australia

First published 1998 in Pan by Pan Macmillan Australia Pty Limited
St Martins Tower, 31 Market Street, Sydney

Copyright © David Dale 1998
Copyright © illustrations Cathy Wilcox 1998

All rights reserved. No part of this book may be reproduced or transmitted in any form or by any means, electronic or mechanical, including photocopying, recording or by any information storage and retrieval system, without prior permission in writing from the publisher.

National Library of Australia Cataloguing-in-Publication data:

Dale, David, 1948– .
The 100 things everyone needs to know about Italy.

ISBN 0 330 36083 3.

1. Italy. I. Title. II. Title: The one hundred things everyone needs to know about Italy.

914.504

Typeset in 10.2/13pt Sabon by Midland Typesetters
Printed in Australia by McPherson's Printing Group

contents

	introduction	vii	27	passegiata	77
1	the place	1	28	soccer	78
2	the people	3	29	other sports	81
3	the must knows	5	30	sex	83
4	the joy of complexity	8	31	cars	85
5	appearances	12	32	design	87
6	the family	14	33	fashion	89
7	the must sees	16	34	how it started	92
8	the must dos	18	35	the middle ages	94
9	the superstars	21	36	the renaissance	96
10	pronunciation	28	37	one nation	99
11	the alphabet	30	38	Mussolini	101
12	languages	32	39	world domination	103
13	phrases	35	40	the economy	105
14	gestures	37	41	big business	107
15	signs	39	42	Berlusconi	109
16	the power structure	42	43	work	112
17	clean hands	45	44	status	114
18	politics	48	45	women	116
19	eating	51	46	gays	118
20	pasta	53	47	marriage	120
21	pizza	56	48	the home	121
22	restaurants	58	49	animals	123
23	the list	62	50	religion	124
24	wine	70	51	the popes	128
25	coffee	73	52	crime	132
26	siesta	75	53	mafias	133

CONTENTS

54 the police	135	79 the other islands	212
55 the legal system	137	80 the other countries	215
56 children	139	81 Milan	217
57 education	141	82 Rome	219
58 health	143	83 Venice	221
59 death	145	84 Florence	223
60 immigration	146	85 Naples	224
61 the papers	148	86 Bologna	226
62 television	150	87 over and under	228
63 cinema	152	88 disasters	230
64 the top films	155	89 weather	232
65 writers	159	90 holidays	234
66 the book	163	91 airports	236
67 art	165	92 hotels	238
68 architecture	168	93 trains	241
69 music	173	94 driving	243
70 opera	176	95 getting around town	245
71 science	179	96 the post office	247
72 firsts	181	97 the phone system	248
73 comedy	185	98 shopping	249
74 campanilismo	187	99 guidebooks	252
75 regions	189	100 next	254
76 Tuscany	197	acknowledgements	255
77 Umbria	202	index	257
78 Sicily	208		

introduction

Italy provokes two reactions among English-speakers: either they become irrationally besotted with it, or they are afraid of it. Both reactions arise from the same suspicion—that the Italians know something we don't; that of all the ways different societies go about the pursuit of happiness, the Italians have got it right.

At any given moment, the hills of Tuscany are alive with the sound of a million Americans, English and Australians trying to find out how to be Italian. Most of them get no further than the food and the art, and return home stimulated but frustrated.

Then there's a second group: the English-speakers who feel threatened by the obvious pleasure Italians take in every aspect of their lives. They fear the anthropologist Luigi Barzini (*The Italians*) may be correct when he says that, in the heart of every human being, 'there is one small corner which is Italian, that part that finds regimentation irksome, the dangers of war frightening, strict morality stifling, that part which loves frivolous and entertaining art, admires larger than life solitary heroes, and dreams of an impossible liberation from the strictures of a tidy existence.' The Protestant

THE 100 THINGS...

mind, which believes that humans need order and discipline, reels at the idea of a society thriving on the edge of chaos.

I'd like to think this book will help both groups, and perhaps even shift group two into group one. Neither group has been well served by the guidebooks on Italy that have been available up to now. Most guidebooks have a lot to say about dead Italians, but mention living Italians only as workers in hotels, restaurants and shops. Their readers are left to float through Italy in a kind of tourist bubble, gaping at the monuments and gulping at the pasta, but understanding nothing of the real life going on around them.

This book contains plenty of history, food, accommodation, even shopping, but that is not its primary purpose. My goal is to enhance your travels—or your memories of travel—by explaining what modern Italians are talking, writing and gesturing about, even if you don't speak a word of the language.

Italians do talk about their art treasures and their food treasures, but they also discuss sex, politics, money, soccer, children, music, clothes, cars and crime. So this book discusses them too.

As far as I know, this is the first book about modern Italy written specifically for Australians. It is designed to be both practical and provocative.

If you want to know how to make a reverse-charges call from Italy, try chapter 97 (phones).

INTRODUCTION

If you want to know why so many Italian prostitutes look like men in drag, try chapter 30 (sex). If you want a list of restaurants that emphasise regional specialities, try chapters 19 to 23. If you wonder why so many streets are called Cavour, Garibaldi and Mazzini, try chapter 37 (one nation). If you arrive in a town and find everything is closed, you may find the explanation in chapter 90 (holidays).

If you're struggling to pronounce a destination or to spell out your name for a hotel booking, try chapters 10 to 14. If you wonder why Italy's entire political system was transformed during the 1990s, try chapter 3 and chapters 16 to 18. If you're stuck in a queue at the post office or the railway station, try chapters 4, 93, and 96, and learn to enjoy every delay.

And if you're planning a visit to a particular city, check its name in the index to learn about its history, its hotels, its restaurants and its politics.

I've travelled to Italy 17 times since my first visit in 1977. I am still trying to find out how, as Barzini puts it, 'Italians seem to understand things which still perplex other people, to have explored short cuts, a few of which are a trifle shabby and questionable, but useful to avoid life's roughest spots ... Italians have mastered the great art of being happy and of making other people happy, an art which embraces and inspires all others in Italy, the only art worth learning, but which can never really be mastered, the art of inhabiting the earth.'

Solving the mystery of Italy is a scholarly pursuit that requires at least one lifetime. I hope you'll join me in the research. And if there turns out to be some fun in it, well, that's the burden we scholars have to bear.

ESSENTIALS

1
the place

Italy has mountains, lakes, and forests; wild bears, boars and wolves; volcanoes, earthquakes and avalanches; and 1600 km of spectacular coastline. Yes, it has Nature. But that's not why you go. The 28 million visitors who arrive each year are there to see what human beings have imposed on those natural assets during the past three thousand years.

The high-heeled boot on the leg of Europe is 1300 km long and 160 km wide; its longest river, the Po, crosses the northern part, while the Apennine mountains run down its length.

It has borders with France, Austria, Switzerland, and Slovenia; to the left is the Tyrrhenian Sea, to the top right is the Adriatic Sea; 23 per cent of it is plains, 42 per cent is hills, and 35 per cent is mountains.

Human beings have cultivated 70 per cent of it; it has a population density of 190 people per sq km (compared with 2 in Australia, 26 in the US, and 327 in Japan); and, with an area of 301,268 sq km, it's a bit bigger than Victoria and less than half the size of New South Wales.

So space is on your side. It should be possible, in

THE 100 THINGS . . .

a lifetime, to see most of the 20 different countries which fit into the boot (or float next to it) and which these days pretend to be part of a united nation called Italy. If you want to understand the 20 Italies as well as just seeing them, this book might help.

ESSENTIALS

2
the people

*i*n 1998, there were 57,103,833 Italians. In 1999, there will be fewer Italians, because the population during the 1990s has been declining by 0.8 per cent a year. In fact, Italy is the oldest country in the world—not because of its monuments, but because 23 per cent of its population is over 65 and only 14 per cent is under 15.

Italians have the highest rate of car ownership in Europe, but the lowest birth rate and the lowest suicide rate (about 8 per 100,000, compared with Australia's rate of 12). They have three times as many shops and twice as many restaurants as the British.

Census figures over the past couple of decades tell us Italians are living longer (male life expectancy 75 years, female life expectancy 82 years, similar to Australia's), having smaller families, growing richer, moving out of the big cities, and shifting their work from farming and heavy industry to the service sector. They are 95 per cent Catholic (though only 35 per cent of them go to church). They have one of the world's lowest rates of heart disease.

Those are a few facts about Italians. Now for a few impressions: Italians are obsessed with food,

THE 100 THINGS ...

clothes, children, hygiene, cars, coffee, conversation, their mothers, soccer, soap operas, luxury, political crises, conspiracies, getting around inconveniences such as the tax laws, and the differences between north and south. They also seem to have found the secret of happiness.

ESSENTIALS

3
the must knows

*t*hese are the names most likely to appear in Italian newspapers and Italian conspiracy theories of the late 1990s:

☆ **ROMANO PRODI.** A jovial economist from Bologna, he became prime minister in 1996 when a coalition of left and centre parties, the Olive Tree, was elected in the wake of corruption allegations that destroyed the ruling parties. To ensure Italy stays within the European currency system, he has the tough job of selling Italians on cutting government spending.

☆ **SILVIO BERLUSCONI.** A billionaire businessman, he became prime minister briefly in 1994 and is now Leader of the Opposition, heading Forza Italia, the biggest party in a conservative coalition called The Freedom Pole. He is facing several trials on bribery charges.

☆ **ANTONIO DI PIETRO.** In 1993, opinion polls showed the tough talker from the hillbilly region of Molise was the most popular man in Italy, because of his pursuit of political corruption as head of the 'Clean Hands' team

THE 100 THINGS . . .

of magistrates. When the Olive Tree coalition was elected in 1996, he was appointed Minister for Public Works, but resigned six months later in protest at being investigated on bribery allegations—set up, he said, by supporters of the politicians he had earlier exposed.

☆ **BETTINO CRAXI.** A Milan lawyer who became leader of the Socialist Party and prime minister in the mid 1980s, he now lives in Tunisia to escape a 20 year jail sentence for seeking bribes. He is Italy's Christopher Skase: claiming to be too ill to attend court, but photographed playing volleyball on a beach.

☆ **SALVATORE 'TOTÒ' RIINA.** The boss of the Sicilian Mafia during the 1980s, he was so ruthless at killing opponents that hundreds of other Cosa Nostra members sought witness protection and gave evidence against him. He is now serving several life sentences.

☆ **UMBERTO BOSSI.** A former medical student and salesman, he heads the Northern League,

which argues that the northern Italians should separate from the south and stop their tax contributions being used to subsidise a bunch of criminals and bums who won't work. He would like to be the founder of a new nation called the Federal Republic of Padania.

☆ **ALDO MORO.** A Christian Democrat prime minister, he was kidnapped and murdered by Red Brigade terrorists in 1978, just as he was about to reach a 'historic compromise' with the Communist Party. His death suited ...

☆ **GIULIO ANDREOTTI.** For 50 years the most powerful person in the Christian Democrat party, he became prime minister in six governments and a cabinet minister in countless others. In the mid 1990s he went on trial for protecting the Mafia (in return for their organising votes for his party) and using them to murder his political opponents.

☆ **LICIO GELLI.** He was the leader of a secret Masonic Lodge called P2, which was found in the early 1980s to have a membership list containing many conservative politicians, public servants and businessmen and to be plotting a right-wing coup. In 1998 Gelli embarrassed the government by mysteriously escaping from house arrest and disappearing.

☆ **ROBERTO BAGGIO.** The nation's top soccer player, he fell from public esteem in 1994 by missing a kick which could have won Italy the World Cup. He now plays for Bologna, and regained some glory with brilliant kicking in the 1998 World Cup series.

PASSIONS

4
the joy of complexity

*t*hree words that describe different generations of European art—byzantine, baroque and rococo—are equally applicable to the way Italians go about their lives. They revel in complexity. Italy is the land that made an art form of red tape, and a million ways to work around it.

The difficulty of getting anything done in Italy may seem surprising in a nation that worships two of life's simplest pleasures: eating well and looking good. Here's a theory: Italians find life so enjoyable that they keep devising unnecessary procedures to make it seem to last longer. And if you're trying to send a parcel in a post office or cash a cheque in a bank or find an official to issue a certificate of residency, life seems to stretch endlessly.

When you do finally send your parcel at the post office, time expands even further. Italians like to tell of a recent case in which some kidnappers in the south sent part of a victim's ear with a ransom note, and had to wait two weeks for it to be delivered to a town 300 km away. They were lucky it was delivered at all.

If those kidnappers were ever caught (by one of Italy's four different police forces, each with its own

PASSIONS

gorgeous uniform), they could look forward to their trials and appeals taking at least ten years, because Italy's courts are clogged by too many laws and too few administrators. Then the kidnappers might find themselves suddenly released as part of an amnesty designed to reduce overcrowding in the jails.

The Italian political system has encouraged a multitude of tiny parties, constantly making and breaking alliances, with the likelihood there'll be a new government every year. The MPs do a lot of fabulous speechmaking, using the gift of the gab which Italians learn because most of their school exams are oral (where verbal skills can cover the absence of knowledge). But what the elected representatives say is irrelevant, since the real running of the country has been done (until recently) by the party officials, who appointed senior public servants on the basis of their loyalty to the party. This was known as *sottogoverno*—'undergovernment'. And because much of the public service was managed by party hacks, it was inefficient and corrupt.

So Italians developed a contempt for their politicians and their public servants which justified tax evasion and bribery: 'Why should my hard-earned money be wasted on supporting those bludgers and crooks, when I could buy my son a flat?' 'Why should I pay a fine for doing an extension to my house when I didn't know the extension was illegal and I can pay the inspector not to report it?' It's estimated that 20 per cent of the economic activity that goes on in Italy is undeclared.

These are some terms to know:

- ☆ *L'arte di arrangiarsi* (lartay di urunj-ussee), literally 'the art of self-managing'. A much admired quality, it could be translated as 'the art of getting away with it'—by whatever it takes to bend the rules.
- ☆ *Carta bollata*, literally 'pre-stamped paper'. It's an official-looking document carrying a few thousand lire worth of stamps, on which you make any declaration or application. It does not make dealing with public servants any faster, but without it, you can't deal with them at all. And it is one way for the government to extract money from the populace.
- ☆ *Ungere* (unjerreh), literally 'to grease'. To get any project through all the permission processes, it helps to hire an agent (*mediatore*) who is expert at negotiating the corridors of the bureaucracy, finding the right forms, the right officials, the right approaches. Just don't ask what he does with all the money you give

him—he is using it to *ungere* the locks on the public service doors.

☆ ***Dietrologia*** (dee-ate-row-lodge-eeya), literally 'behindology', the conviction that nothing is as it seems. Italians know there are conspiracies everywhere.

Thus the Red Brigades might have looked like left-wing terrorists but they were actually a front for right-wingers in the security agencies who wanted to create an unstable atmosphere which would let them stage a military coup. The Vatican is in there somewhere too, since its bankers got tied up with the Mafia. (You don't think the original Pope John Paul died of natural causes, do you?) And Giulio Andreotti, former Christian Democrat party leader, may be on trial for murdering a political opponent and using the Mafia to organise votes in Sicily, but really it's a CIA plot to discredit him because his Catholic conservatism is a handicap now that the Cold War is over.

The joy of *dietrologia* is that once you've found the plot behind the plot, you must seek the plot behind *that*! With any luck, you can keep talking about it for years. After all, talking is the greatest pleasure of all.

5
appearances

*t*he average Italian spends $3,000 a year on clothes—twice the average for the rest of Europe and three times the average for Australia. This statistic is a manifestation of the concern with *bella figura*—beautiful image.

It's vital to present yourself to the world as self-confident, wealthy and tasteful, even if you are none of those things. Maybe you can only afford one jacket, but if it's an Armani, you can wear it every day. What matters is that everyone notices *la firma*—the label. Another translation of *bella figura* might be 'keeping up appearances'.

If you think of Italian men as wearing shirts unbuttoned to the waist with an array of gold chains around the neck and wrists, you're thinking about an American Mafia soldier, not an Italian. An Italian man is more likely to be wearing a dark suit and a tie. That will cover his one piece of jewellery—a slim gold chain around the neck, occasionally with a cross or an image of a favourite saint. If he is also wearing a gold wrist bracelet, he is probably from the south.

A man with a beard is signalling that he is an academic, or active in a cause such as ecology.

PASSIONS

When he wants to look casual, the Italian male drapes an expensive sweater round his shoulders, with the sleeves loosely tied at chest level, and wears very expensive shoes without socks. He never wears shorts.

One in three Italian women (7.7 million) has a fur coat, and she'll wear it often at night, even in summer. Women don't overdo the jewellery—one ring, one bracelet, one pearl necklace or gold chain, one set of earrings. On formal occasions they're unlikely to dress in the latest fashions from Milan— more likely the enduringly elegant lines from a couple of years past.

Bella figura is also established by acts of extreme generosity. When a friend's child is born, give it a very expensive gold chain. When invited to dinner (usually at a restaurant, with the host paying for everyone), bring a present for the host that is worth more than what you'd pay for the meal.

Anglos can never have *bella figura*, no matter how many Milan clothes they buy. The best an Anglo can do is be neat and clean. That, at least, will avoid Italy's worst possible condemnation: *brutta figura*, which we might translate as 'dagginess'.

6
the family

*t*hink of the Italian family as an inverted pyramid. At the wide top is a bunch of grandparents and grand uncles and aunts, all determined to be helpful in the upbringing of their grandchild. In the middle is the married couple (and their brothers, sisters and cousins) with a constant supply of free babysitters. And at the bottom—the point of it all—is one child, carrying the weight of all the love and attention from above.

In the 1950s, the Italian family would have been more like a cube, with almost as many children at the bottom as there were grand-relatives at the top. Back then, Italy had a birthrate of about 3 children per woman. Nowadays, Italy has the lowest birthrate in the world—1.2 children per woman, which compares with 1.8 in Britain and Australia, and is well behind the long-term replacement rate of 2.1. The cause, says the Catholic Church, is selfishness.

The reduction in size has not made the Italian family any less closely knit. Those pyramids are the building blocks of Italian society, the support network that compensates for all inefficiencies in social services. The Anglo-Saxon world emphasises the individual. Italian society emphasises the family

ICONS

unit. Nearly 90 per cent of private businesses in Italy are family-run. Nepotism is not a sin, it's an obligation.

While Anglo teenagers look forward to moving out of home and living with other young people, most Italian kids are reconciled to staying with their parents (and often their grandparents, too) till they marry. Some 80 per cent of Italians between 14 and 29 are still living 'at home'.

Once married, most couples stay with the parents of one partner until the whole family has put together enough money to help them buy an apartment, which, ideally, will be in the same street as one of the parental homes. And then they'll go ahead and have their one child (usually named after the paternal grandfather, if it's a boy).

The words to know are: *mammismo* (the Italian boy's love of his mother, who reciprocates by cooking, washing and cleaning for him long after he is married); *mammoni* (mother's boys, which is what most Italian men proudly are); *pa* and *ma* (what Italian kids call their parents, while grandparents are called *nonno* and *nonna*), and *un single* (a word Italians had to borrow for that rare phenomenonon, an unmarried person living alone).

ICONS

7
the must sees

*h*ere are ten things all visitors to Italy should have seen before they declare their journeyings over:

1. The Grand Canal in Venice, best experienced by taking the slow vaporetto (No. 1) from the railway station to the public gardens.
2. *The Last Supper*, by Leonardo Da Vinci, on the wall of the monks' canteen attached to Santa Maria delle Grazie church in Milan.
3. The statue of Moses, by Michelangelo, in the church of San Pietro in Vincoli (St Peter in Chains) in Rome. Moses, who has horns, is angrily trying to drag himself out of a block of marble.
4. The Fantiscritti quarries in the marble mountains of Carrara, Tuscany, where Michelangelo chose the blocks that made his sculptures.
5. Monte Solaro in Capri (reached by a gently swinging chairlift over orchards), which offers a panorama of southern Italy, including the Bay of Naples and the hills of Calabria.
6. The 2,000 year-old fast food takeaway stores in Via dell'Abbondanza, Pompeii.

7. The monastery on which Umberto Eco's book *The Name of the Rose* was based: Sacra di San Michele, a labyrinthine stone structure built in the 11th century on a clifftop above Avigliana, west of Turin.
8. The catacombs of the Convento dei Cappuccini (not a coffee bar), in Palermo, where 8,000 corpses, in varying stages of decomposition and sorted by profession, are propped up in elegant tableaux.
9. The walls of Lucca, Tuscany, built 400 years ago and thick enough for their top to be a walking track and children's playground stretching four kilometres.
10. Mount Etna, Sicily, which should be climbed at night so you can look down into blackness and see the glowing heart of a live volcano.

ICONS

8
the must dos

*h*ere are ten activities that will help you understand the Italians:

1. Spend a night channel-surfing through television. You'll encounter a bevy of bimbo presenters, inane game shows, dubbed American soap operas, singing contests, ancient documentaries, kitsch shopping opportunities and discussion programs with intellectuals debating arcane issues.
2. Climb the 486 steps inside the leaning Asinelli Tower in Bologna and, from the top, survey the roofs of the city known as *la rossa* (the red). The nickname comes partly from Bologna's colouring but mainly from its politics, which represent the world's only successful blend of hedonism and communism.
3. See a movie called *Yesterday, Today and Tomorrow*, in which Sophia Loren and Marcello Mastroianni display three facets of the Italian personality: Neapolitan cunning, Roman cheerfulness, and Milanese cool.
4. Go to a soccer match on a Sunday afternoon—ideally a match involving Juventus or Bologna

ICONS

if you want to see flashing footwork, but mainly to observe the enthusiasm of the *tifosi* (fans).

5. Go window shopping around Milan's Piazza San Babila, observing design stores such as Morongomma and Arflex, and fashion houses such as Versace and Krizia, to discover how Milan defines Style for the world.
6. Read Dante's *The Divine Comedy* in English translation. Not only is it the book that every Italian has studied at school, but it was the basis for much of the Western world's comedy and drama.
7. Have lunch in the dining car of an Italian train—for example, the Vesuvio from Bologna to Milan (leaving at 1.42, arriving at 3.40) or the less romantically named ES9443 from Venice to Florence (leaving at 11.48, arriving at 2.32). The food will be pretty good, the ever-changing scenery will be inspiring and the rituals (waiters asking if you want gassy or non-gassy mineral water, Italians eating their fruit with a knife and fork) will be instructive.

8. Buy a copy of the paparazzi magazine *Eva Tremila*, and

ponder Italy's preoccupation with semi-nude starlets, gambling and adultery.
9. Drink two glasses of Tignanello wine (it will be at least $70 a bottle in Italy, but twice that outside), and discover that Italy can produce reds which approach the greatness of Grange or Chateau Petrus.
10. Throw a 100 lire coin (before they are replaced by Eurocurrency) into Rome's Trevi fountain—corny, but if you don't, you might never come back.

ICONS

9
the superstars

*t*hese are the world's most talked-about Italians, for better or worse ...

- ☆ **ROMULUS AND REMUS**, originators. Legend has it they were descendants of Aeneas (a son of the goddess Venus who moved to Italy after the Greeks sacked his home town of Troy). They were brought up by a she-wolf before founding the city of Rome in 753 BC. Romulus killed Remus, starting a tradition of political backstabbing.
- ☆ **GAIUS JULIUS CAESAR**, dictator. Born in Rome in 100 BC, he became a successful military commander (conquering Gaul, Germany, Britain, Spain, Egypt, and northern Africa), lover (Cleopatra bore him a son), author (he wrote histories of his military campaigns), jurist, orator, mapmaker, and architect. He was made dictator for life in 45 BC, with his face on coins and a month named after him, but was assassinated in 44 BC.
- ☆ **NERO CLAUDIUS CAESAR**, politician. Born in 37 AD and appointed Roman emperor in 54 AD, he murdered his mother, his step-brother

and two wives, recited poetry while Rome was nearly destroyed in a fire, tortured Christians, and plundered the empire to pay for extravagant building projects. He committed suicide in 68 AD after being overthrown by the army.

☆ **DANTE ALIGHIERI**, poet. Born 1265, son of a Florence lawyer, he fell in love with a girl named Beatrice when he and she were nine, and couldn't stop writing about her (though they never even kissed). He became a local administrator in Florence, then ambassador to Rome. He is best known for the epic poem *The Divine Comedy*, a vision of hell, purgatory and heaven and a commentary on his times. By writing in the Tuscan dialect instead of Latin, he set down the language which became modern Italian.

☆ **THE MEDICI**, politicians. They were a Florentine dynasty founded by a banker named Giovanni de Medici around 1400. His son Cosimo became ruler of Florence, builder of grand projects and patron of the arts. The big names in the family were Lorenzo (The Magnificent), a poet and political operator who discovered Michelangelo; Catharine, who married the heir to the French throne in 1533 (aged 14) and introduced the French to Italian cooking; Giovanni, who became Pope Leo X in 1513 and said, 'God has given us the papacy, now let us enjoy it'; Cosimo I, who was named Grand Duke of Tuscany by the Pope in 1569, making the family hereditary rulers; Cosimo II, who protected Galileo from being executed by the Church in 1633; and Gian Gastone, a slob who ended the Medici line when he died in the Pitti Palace in 1737.

☆ **THE BORGIAS**, politicians. Pope Alexander VI (real name Rodrigo Borgia) had various children by various mistresses, but two are remembered: Cesare, who led a papal army to conquer most of central Italy in 1499 and, with the motto 'Either Caesar or nothing', arranged the assassinations of a string of political opponents; and Lucrezia, who helped her brother Cesare murder her husband in 1500 and then married Alfonso d'Este, duke of Ferrara, where she became a patron of the arts.

☆ **NICCOLO MACHIAVELLI**, author. An adviser to Cesare Borgia and an administrator of Florence in the early 16th century, he is remembered for writing *Seven Books on the Art of War*, a satirical play called *La Mandragola*, and a cynical self-help text called *The Prince* which offers advice on gaining and holding power.

☆ **LEONARDO DA VINCI**, artist/engineer. Born in 1452 near Pisa and trained as a painter, he moved to Milan and became a court artist for the Sforza family, returning to Florence to work as an engineer for Cesare Borgia, and then to Amboise, France, to work as an artist for King Louis XII. He is remembered for his scientific drawings and writings, for a wall decoration called *The Last Supper* (1498), and for a painting called *Mona Lisa* (1504).

☆ **CRISTOFORO COLOMBO**, explorer. Born in Genoa in 1451, he went to sea at the age of 14, and spent years trying to persuade various European rulers to help him reach India by sailing westwards. In 1492, the Spanish rulers Ferdinand and Isabella financed an expedition which ultimately landed at islands now known as the Bahamas, the West Indies, Haiti and Cuba.

☆ **MICHELANGELO BUONAROTTI**, artist. Born in 1475 near Florence, brought up by a stonemason, he joined a team of artists at the court of Lorenzo the Magnificent of Florence, then worked on various commissions for Pope Julius II in Rome. The original Renaissance man, he was a poet, painter, sculptor, military engineer and architect, best known for the statue of David, the ceiling of the Sistine Chapel, and the design of St Peter's Basilica.

☆ **GALILEO GALILEI**, astronomer. Born in Pisa in 1564, he became professor of mathematics at Pisa University and theorised that all falling bodies, large or small, descend at the same speed. He perfected the telescope, and after studying the night sky, demonstrated that the earth revolves round the sun—a view which got him sentenced to prison by the Catholic Church. After intervention by the Duke of Tuscany, he was allowed to retire to Florence, where he died in 1642.

☆ **ANTONIO VIVALDI**, composer. Born in Venice in 1678, he was priest and choirmaster at the church of Santa Maria della Pieta until he had an affair with a soprano and had to move to Vienna. Best known in his lifetime for a multitude of concertos, he influenced the baroque music of Bach, and was revived in the 20th century because of the popularity of *Le Quattro Stagione* (*The Four Seasons*).

☆ **GIUSEPPE VERDI**, composer. Born near Busseto in north central Italy in 1813, and trained as a church organist, he became Italy's greatest opera composer, best known for *Rigoletto*, *La Traviata*, and *Aida*.

☆ **GIUSEPPE GARIBALDI**, campaigner. Born in Nice in 1807, he was first a sailor, then a fighter for the unification of the various countries within the peninsula into one nation called Italy. In 1859 Garibaldi and a thousand red-shirted troops sailed from Genoa to Sicily, defeated the local forces and then sailed on to Naples, which they claimed for the King of Piemonte (the region which had initiated the unification struggle). King Vittore Emmanuele II

THE 100 THINGS . . .

of Piemonte became the first King of Italy.

☆ **BENITO MUSSOLINI**, politician. Born near Forli, central Italy, in 1883, he founded the fascism movement, and was dictator of Italy from 1922 to 1943, when he was overthrown by his governing council because Italy was losing the war. He was executed in Milan in 1945.

☆ **FEDERICO FELLINI**, film-maker. Born in 1920 in Rimini, he was a journalist and cartoonist before becoming a director in the late 1940s. He is best known for eccentric humour and social satire, as in *La Dolce Vita* (1960), *8½* (1963), *Satyricon* (1969) and *Amarcord* (1974).

☆ **LUCIANO PAVAROTTI**, singer. Born in Modena in 1935, he made his US debut in 1964 in *Lucia Di Lammermoor* with Joan Sutherland, and went on to become the world's most famous tenor, collaborating with two Spaniards in The Three Tenors, and singing Puccini's 'Nessun Dorma' at the 1990 World Cup soccer final in Rome.

☆ **SOPHIA LOREN**, actress. Born in Rome in 1934, she symbolises the sensuous Italian woman, in movies such as *Yesterday, Today and Tomorrow* and *Two Women*, for which she won an Oscar.

☆ **UMBERTO ECO**. Born in Allesandria, near Turin, in 1929, he is Professor of Semiotics at Bologna University, a commentator on popular culture and the author of *The Name of the Rose*, a bestselling murder mystery, and *Foucault's Pendulum*, which was too clever for its own good.

☆ **MARCELLA HAZAN**, cook. Born in 1935, Venice-based but highly Americanised, she has become the international voice of Italian food, from her *Classic Italian Cookbook* in the mid 1970s to *Marcella Cucina* in the late 1990s.

☆ **CICCIOLINA**, porn actress. Born in Hungary in the 1960s (real name Ilona Staller), she moved to Italy as a teenager and began doing sex talk shows on radio and nude appearances on TV. In 1987 she was elected to parliament as an MP for the Radical party on an anti-nuclear and sexual liberation policy, and served until 1992. During the 1991 Gulf War, she offered to sleep with Saddam Hussein if he would cease fighting.

COMMUNICATION

10
pronunciation

*M*ost Italians are happy to try a bit of English for a traveller who doesn't speak Italian, but it helps communication if you can approximate their pronunciation. Asking the way to Chioggia (near Venice), for example, you would be met with blank stares if you said the word the way it looks in English. It is pronounced 'key-odge-uh'. Ordering grilled fish (*pesce alla griglia*) you'd better ask for 'pesh-eh ulluh grilya', or you might end up with burnt peaches.

Unlike English, where there is little logical relationship between spelling and pronunciation, Italian follows simple rules. And while many letters in English words make no sound at all (through? psychology?), every letter in an Italian word enters into its pronounciation. Thus the often-used term *cioé* ('that is to say') might come out sounding like 'sew' in English, but in Italian it sounds like 'chee-oh-eh'.

When you need to read an Italian word aloud, or write down something said to you, these principles might help . . .

☆ The letter e is pronounced like the e in bed.

COMMUNICATION

The letter **i** is pronounced like ee in feet.

☆ The combination **ch**, as in zucchini, is always pronounced 'k'.

☆ The letter 'c' is pronounced 'k' if it's before a, o, u or h. It's pronounced 'ch' if it's before e or i. Thus the word for house (*casa*) is pronounced 'kahzuh', and the word for hi! (*ciao*) is pronounced 'chow'.

☆ The letter **g** is pronounced hard (as in get) if it's before a, o, u, or h, and soft (as in job) if it's before e or i. Thus the name Giorgio is pronounced 'jaw-joe', while you put a 'jet-oh-neh' (*gettone*) in a public phone.

☆ The combination **glia** is always pronounced 'lya', as in the pasta *tagliatelle* ('tulyuh-tell-eh') or in the cooking method *alla griglia* ('grilya').

A useful word on which to test your skills is *chiacchiere*, which are pastries you might get with coffee (literal meaning: chattering). Try it before you read on. You should have come out with something like 'kee-yuk-yeah-reh'.

COMMUNICATION

11
the alphabet

*t*here will be times as a traveller in Italy when you will have to spell your name or listen to others spelling the names of places or people. So it's handy to know the Italian alphabet, which turns out to be the same as the English alphabet, except that it contains no J, K, W, X or Y. The j sound is represented by the letter g (*giornale*—journal). The k sound is spelt c in front of a, o, or u (*casa*—house) or ch in front of other vowels (*chianti*). Thus the word for cooking, *cucina*, is pronounced 'koo-cheena'. The Y sound is spelt either as i or gl (*tagliatelle*, the flat noodle pronounced 'tulyuh-tell-eh').

Here's how the alphabet is spoken, and the standard words that Italians use to make the letters clear:

ah (Ancona)
bee (Bologna)
chee (Como)
dee (Domodossola)
e—as in 'head' (Empoli)
effeh (Firenze)
gee (Grosseto)

COMMUNICATION

ahka (Hotel)
ee (Imola)
elleh (Livorno)
emmeh (Milano)
enneh (Napoli)
o—as in 'pot' (Otranto)
pee (Palermo)
koo (Quattro)
erreh (Roma)
esseh (Savona)
tee (Taranto)
oo (Udine)
voo (Vicenza)
zeta (Zara)

Okay then, what if your name is Jay Wilkes? Most Italians are aware of the peculiar excesses of the English alphabet, and have names for the surplus letters. A hotel clerk would understand if you spell it 'ee-lungo, ah, ipsilon, doppio voo, ee, elleh, kappa, e, esseh'. And 'icks' will mark the spot for the 24th letter, as long as you don't use it in espresso.

COMMUNICATION

12
languages

*M*odern Italian is the evolution of the Latin spoken by the ancient Romans (a language which also generated about half the words in English and most of French and Spanish). But Latin evolved differently in different parts of the peninsula, and the form called *Italiano standard*, which is now taught in schools and used by the mass media, is actually the Tuscan dialect first written down in the 14th century by the authors Dante, Petrarch and Bocaccio.

In 1861, when the country was first unified, only 1 in 10 Italians actually spoke the Tuscan form. Now, thanks to the standardising efforts of Mussolini and the media, six out of seven Italians speak it (in addition to their local dialect).

Dialect lets an Italian identify where another Italian comes from (and judge them according to regional stereotype). North-easterners tend to drop the last vowel off words, so that *pane* ('pah-neh', bread) becomes 'pan', and *treno* (train) becomes 'tren'. They pronounce 't' as 'd' (fradello not *fratello*) and hard 'c' as hard 'g' (gasa not *casa*), while the soft c which Tuscans pronounce 'ch' sounds more like 's' in the north (sitta, not *citta*).

North-eastern dialect is not uniform: even cities as close as Venice, Padua and Vicenza have different words for 'today': respectively, *ancuo*, *inco*, and *onco*. The word in *Italiano standard* is *oggi*.

People in Tuscany tend to say the 'k' sound as if it were an 'h', and are often parodied with the phrase 'hoha-hola hon la hannucia' which means 'Coca-Cola with a straw' (written *Coca-Cola con la cannuccia*). A 'c' before i or e sounds more like 'sh' than the 'ch' of *Italiano standard*, so that *bacio* (kiss) is 'basho' rather than bah-che-oh. Tuscan has a lilt that can sound Spanish.

People from Sicily say the 'll' sound as 'dd', so *capelli* (hair) sounds more like 'capiddi'. Like the northerners, they tend to drop vowels off the ends of nouns, and in some combinations they make p sound like b ('combrare', to buy, rather than *comprare*) and s sound like z ('inzlata', salad, not *insalata*).

Neapolitans have the most vigorous and scatological dialect. Their way of referring to heavy rain is '*Chiove, chiove, che cagamento i cazzo!*' (literally 'it's raining, it's raining, it's shitting on my dick').

In Sicily, the sound written as 'gi' (usually pronounced 'j') sounds like 'sh', so Giorgio becomes 'shore-show'. The Sicilian vocabulary varies considerably, too, so that the word for 'then' is *tann*, not *allora* and the word for 'above' is *ngopp* not *sopra*.

Italy's linguistic variations don't stop at dialects. In the Val d'Aosta you'll mainly hear Provençal French spoken (and even down as far as Genoa, French words appear in the dialect). In Trentino you'll hear a lot of German. Some parts of Puglia and Calabria speak Greek or Albanian. In Sardinia they speak a form of Catalan.

But then again, English is a highly fashionable language, and Italians everywhere have adopted into their standard vocabulary such terms as barbecue, body building, boyfriend, chewing gum, disc jockey, fast food, gay, gadget, hamburger, hi tech, jazz, picnic, quiz, star, trend, and yuppie.

COMMUNICATION

13
phrases

*i*t's a good idea to carry a paperback dictionary in Italy (I find *Harrap's* pretty good), but here's a short list of terms that may get you out of difficulties.

Hello: *Buongiorno* (Bwon-jor-noh). *Ciao* is only for good friends.

Do you speak English?: *Parla Inglese?* (parluh in-glazy?).

How do you get to ...?: *Come si arriva a ...?* (commeh see urrivuh uh ...?)

Where is ...?: *Dov'è?* (doh-veh?)

Do you have?: *Ha?* (uh?)

I would like ...: *Vorrei* (vorray)

This: *Questo* (kwesto)

Two of these: *Due di questi* (doo-eh dee kwest-ee).

You (polite): *lei* (lay-ee).

How much is it?: *Quanto è?* (kwunto eh?)

What would you like?: *Che cosa desidera?* (Kay kohzuh dezideruh?)

I'm just looking: *Sto solo guardando* (sto solo gwar-dundo)

I don't understand: *Non capisco* (non capeeskoh)

More slowly: *Piu lentamente* (peeyu lent-uh-ment-eh).

What is this called in Italian?: *Come si dice in*

THE 100 THINGS ...

Italiano? (com-eh see dee-cheh in Italiano?)

Can you write it down?: *Puo scriverlo?* (poo-oh scree-verloh?)

Please: *Per favore* (pair fuh-voreh)

Thank you: *Grazie* (Graht-zee-eh)

You're welcome: *Prego* (pray-goh). It also means 'Can I help you?' and 'Go ahead'.

I'd like to book ... *Vorrei prenotare* ... (voray prayno-tahreh) a room: *una camera*, a table: *un tavolo*.

My name is: *Il mio nome e* (eel meeyo nomeh eh)

I come from Australia: *Vengo dall'Australia* (vengo dull ah-oo-strah-lee-yuh)

Fuck off: *Vaffanculo* (vuffungooloh)

Goodbye: *Arrivederci* (uh-ree-vedair-chee)

You know you're being insulted if an Italian throws these words at you: *asino* (donkey), *bestia* (beast), *cazzone* (prick), *coglione* (testicle), *figlio di un cane* (son of a dog), *frocio* (homosexual), *imbecille* (imbecile), *ladro* (thief), *merda* (shit), *mostro* (monster), *pazzo* (mad), *puttana* (whore), *stronzo* (turd), *testa di cazzo* (dickhead), *ubriaco* (drunkard), *verme* (worm), *la tipica fredezza anglo-sassone* (typical Anglo Saxon coldness).

You know you've made a good impression if an Italian uses these words: *amore mio* (my love), *anima mia* (my soul), *bistecchina* (little steak), *coniglietto* (bunny), *fragolina* (little strawberry), *gucci-pucci* (gitchy gitchy goo), *micio* (kitten), *tesoro* (my treasure), *zuccherino* (little sugar).

RITUALS

14
gestures

*j*ust as an Anglo can never achieve *bella figura*, an Anglo is always going to look a bit silly trying to make gestures the way Italians do. But as you watch Italians communicating, this advice might help you recognise what they are trying to say ...

Flicking the chin outwards with the top of the hand means 'I don't like it' or 'Count me out'.

Swivelling the right hand up and down means 'so-so' or 'not so bad, not so good'.

Two hands on forehead means 'Mamma mia'.

Pulling back two hands, palms outwards, towards the shoulders means 'I'll have nothing to do with it'.

Kissing fingers or making an O shape with the thumb and forefinger means 'excellent'.

Rubbing the fingers against the thumb means 'How much?' or 'What do you want really?'

Tapping the side of the nose with the forefinger means 'in the know' or 'a word to the wise'.

Raising the forefinger and the little finger like horns means 'cuckold' if the fingers are pointed upwards, and 'heaven forbid' (warding off bad luck) if the hand is pointing downwards. Touching

THE 100 THINGS ...

the testicles is also a sign of reassurance, warding off bad luck.

Raising the chin so the head tilts back means 'I don't know' or 'Perhaps I know but I won't tell you'.

Left hand on right bicep, raising right fist means 'Get fucked'.

COMMUNICATION

15
signs

*t*he word *graffiti* comes from the Latin verb 'to scratch', and the Italians have been at it for millennia. More than 3000 messages have been deciphered on the walls of Pompeii, written during the 200 years before the volcano struck. They include the personal: 'O Chiusa, I hope that your ulcerous pustules reopen and burn even more than they did before'; the political: 'Vote for Lucius Popidius Sabinus. His grandmother worked hard for his last election and is pleased with the results'; the philosophical: 'No-one is a gentleman who has not loved a woman'; the ironic: 'I am surprised, o wall, that you, who have to bear the weariness of so many writers, are still standing'; and the prophetic: 'Nothing in the world can endure forever'.

Standards have slipped since 79 AD. To make sense of modern graffiti, you need to know that the letter 'W' or 'M' in front of a name means *Viva* or 'Up with', while *Abbasso* means 'Down with', usually followed by a different soccer team name. These days you might see *Prodi Pinocchio* (a reference to the current prime minister having promised not to raise taxes before the 1996 election) or

THE 100 THINGS ...

Andreotti Mafia (an allegation against a former Prime Minister). If you see a rubbish bin inscribed *Sede CCD*, the graffitist is trying to say that the bin is party headquarters for the Christian Democrats.

Then there are the official signs, to be found on doorways, windows and poles as well as walls. Here's a selection ...

Albergo: hotel
Aperto: open
Arrivi: arrivals
Bancomat: ATM
Biglietteria: ticket office
Binario: platform
Cambio: money exchange
Chiuso: closed
Fermata: bus stop (or tram stop)
FS or Ferroviaria: railway station
Gabinetti: toilets
Guasto: broken (as on a public phone)
Ingresso gratuito: free admission
Messa In Corso: service in progress (in a church)
Parcheggio: parking
Partenze: departures
Pronto Soccorso: casualty (in a hospital)
Questura: police station
Reclamo Bagagli: baggage claim
Riservato Ai Disabili: reserved for disabled
Sciopero: strike
Senso Unico: one way

COMMUNICATION

Sosta Vietata: no parking
Spingere: push
Tirare: pull
Uscita: way out
Vendesi: for sale
Vietato Fumare/Flash/Toccare: no smoking/using flash/touching
Voli Internazionali: international flights
Voli Interni: flights within Italy

RITUALS

16
the power structure

*I*taly has been a nation only since 1860, when a variety of principalities got together under one king (who had previously just been the King of Piedmont, near Genoa). In a referendum on 2 June, 1946, Italians voted narrowly to get rid of the king and become a republic. They'd had 21 years of dictatorship (with royal approval) and six years of war, and they were ready for a change. (All male heirs of the last king are banned from setting foot in Italy, although the current claimant, Victor Emmanuel, lives in Geneva hoping for the law to be changed.)

Nowadays the most powerful person in Italy is, in theory, the president, who is chosen for a seven-year term by an electoral college made up of members of both houses of parliament plus three delegates from each of Italy's 20 regions. The man chosen in 1992 was Oscar Scalfaro.

The president has a lot of symbolic functions, but his key role is appointing a prime minister by judging which member of parliament is likely to control the most votes in the chamber of deputies. This keeps the president pretty busy, since Italian governments have been changing, on average, once a year since

RITUALS

1947. That doesn't mean an election every year, just that the various parties which make up the governing coalitions keep having disputes, which cause the prime minister to resign and ask the president to resolve the matter. Often the president does this by appointing the same person prime minister again.

The prime minister, formally known as the *Presidente del Consiglio* (conseelyo) appoints a cabinet, the *Consiglio dei Ministri*.

There are two houses of parliament: the senate, with 326 members serving five-year terms, and the chamber of deputies, with 630 members serving five-year terms. In both houses most MPs are directly elected by local constituencies, but one fifth are added according to a formula which ensures proportional representation for Italy's regions.

Everyone over 18 votes for the chamber of

deputies, while only people over 25 vote for the senate, presumably because age brings wisdom to the house of review. Italian politicians are among the best paid in the world. A backbench MP earns more than 130 million lire a year, and gets free train travel and free use of telephones for life.

Beneath the national government are three more tiers of government—regional, provincial and communal. There are 20 regional governments, with power over tourism, roads and health care. Then there are 94 provincial governments, which issue car number plates and otherwise seem to duplicate either the regional or the local government. The most personal representation is at the level of the commune, which can be a town or part of a town. The council is called *la giunta* (joonta) *communale*, headed by *il sindaco*—the mayor. All of these smaller forms of government contain the same dazzling array of parties that feature in the central government, and are subject to the same processes of coalition, dissension and collapse.

All tiers of government are forced to listen to a collection of influential pressure groups: three trade union organisations (CGIL on the left, CISL in the centre and UIL on the right), two business lobbies (Confindustria and Confcommercio), two farming groups (Confcoltivatori, Confagricoltura) and, of course, the Roman Catholic Church, though its influence has waned since it lost the fight against the legalisation of divorce and abortion.

TRANSFORMATIONS

17
clean hands

*i*n early 1992, Mario Chiesa (key-aze-uh), a senior member of the Socialist party in Milan, was publicly accused by his ex-wife of taking bribes from businesses seeking government contracts. Under investigation by a local magistrate named Antonio Di Pietro, Chiesa named 700 people who had received *tangenti* (bribes) from businesses in Milan. The bribes were mostly not for personal use. They were sought on behalf of political parties, supposedly to help in running election campaigns.

A can of worms flew open, as businessmen rushed to tell the authorities how they had been subject to political extortion for years. Graffiti artists in Milan wrote *Benvenuti a Tangentopoli* (Welcome to Bribesville) on the walls. Soon the evidence suggested that Rome was just as much of a *tangentopoli* as Milan, and that all the major political parties were demanding donations from business in return for favourable treatment in the allocation of government contracts. It was estimated that from the early 1980s to the early 1990s, 17,000 billion lire ($17 billion) went round in bribes, meticulously divided up by the party bureaucrats. The effect was to inflate the cost of all government purchases, because the businesses simply added the cost of doing business this way onto their charges.

Antonio Di Pietro became a national hero as he led a team of magistrates in a massive investigation called *Mani Pulite*, or Clean Hands. The first person convicted, Mario Chiesa, was sentenced to jail for six years and fined six billion lire (about $6 million).

Within five years, 5000 people, including 300 members of the Italian parliament, were charged with crimes connected with *Tangentopoli*. No-one was immune, not even Italy's biggest private companies Fiat and Olivetti, both of which admitted paying bribes, and not even former prime ministers: the Socialist leader Bettino Craxi was convicted of bribery and fraud and disappeared to Tunisia before he could be jailed; Christian Democrat Ciriaco De Mita was accused of diverting into his party's coffers billions of lire intended for earthquake relief.

The result of the investigation was the removal of Italy's entire ruling class within two years. The Christian Democrat party and the Socialist party fell apart, some of their MPs joining other parties and some retiring to wait for their jail sentences.

But by the mid 1990s, the power of Clean Hands began to wane. Some of the magistrates on the team recommended publicly that the investigation should be wound up. Di Pietro resigned after his political enemies tried to frame him on a charge of taking a bribe to drop an investigation. The courts have huge

TRANSFORMATIONS

backlogs of bribery charges, and some cases look like lasting well into the 21st century. The new government decided in 1997 that people sentenced to jail terms of less than three years would not need to actually go to jail, in order to avoid overcrowding.

RITUALS

18
politics

*b*etween 1947 and 1994, Italy had a multitude of political parties perpetually falling in and out of coalition. But only two parties actually mattered: the Christian Democrats (*Democrazia Cristiana*), who always controlled the government, and the Communists, who always dominated the opposition.

The Christian Democrats had been set up just after World War II with the backing of the Catholic Church and the US Government to keep the communists out of power, even though Italy's version of communism was about as left-wing as Britain's Labour Party. During 40 years the Christian Democrats created a seemingly permanent ruling elite with a network of corruption that spread through every aspect of Italian life.

But in the 1990s, everything turned upside down. The Communist Party disbanded itself in 1990, and some of its former members set up the Democratic Party of the Left (*Partito Democratico della Sinistra*) based on the humane form of socialism which had operated in the city of Bologna. Two referendums changed the voting system to limit the way fringe parties could gain seats with a tiny share of the vote. And the Clean Hands investigation showed Italians that political corruption had gone way beyond their broad limits of tolerance. The Christian Democrats fragmented into seven small parties. The Socialist Party disappeared. An organisation called the Northern League (*Lega Nord*) gained votes by calling for the hardworking north to secede from the lazy south.

In 1993 a Milan media mogul named Silvio Berlusconi created a new party called *Forza Italia* (Go Italy!—the slogan shouted from the stands at international soccer games). It gained a third of the votes in the 1994 election and was able to form a coalition with the Northern League, plus some of the old Christian Democrats and a neo-fascist party called the National Alliance. But the coalition collapsed after the Clean Hands magistrates placed Berlusconi under investigation for paying bribes to advance some of his business interests.

In the 1996 elections the Democratic Party of the Left got the largest share of the vote, and formed a coalition called *l'Ulivo* (the Olive Tree) with the Greens, the Popular Party (a centrist group of former Christian Democrats), and a leftish group called Italian Renewal. The Olive Tree was an inspired name—for

Italians it has connotations of comfort, flavour, and health. Their chosen prime minister was a Bolognese economist (and former Christian Democrat) named Romano Prodi.

Berlusconi now leads an opposition grouping called the Freedom Pole (*Polo Della Liberta*), linking his Forza Italia with the National Alliance and some fragments of the Christian Democrats. He is seen as a short-term opposition leader, likely to be replaced by the charming Gianfranco Fini, leader of the National Alliance. Fini claims the AN has cast aside its fascist origins.

The Northern League stays stubbornly out of both groupings, and votes with whoever seems to be advancing the interests of the north. Another party called the Refounded Communists mostly votes with l'Ulivo. Romano Prodi hopes Italy is moving towards a Westminster two-party system, and predicts there won't be an election until the due date of 2001. If he's right, it would mean political stability unprecedented in Italy's history.

CONSUMPTION

19
eating

*t*here is no such thing as Italian cooking, because the peninsula and its islands contain at least 20 different national cuisines. The polenta-and-butter-based cooking of Milan is as different from the pasta-and-oil-based cooking of Sicily as French food is from Greek. One of the pleasures of travelling in Italy is being constantly confronted with new approaches to life's most important activity.

There are, however, a few generalisations that can be made about the Italian way of eating ...

First, they are no good at breakfast (*prima colazione*). They start the day standing up at a bar with a *cappuccino* and a *cornetto* (sweet roll), saving their appetites for *pranzo* (lunch). It's usual to pay for the *caffe e cornetto* in advance at the cash desk, getting a *scontrino* (ticket) to give to the coffee maker. Some hotels make a token effort for travellers, providing a buffet of cereals and tea bags with almost-boiling water. But a true traveller gets into the mood of the country from the moment of waking.

Lunch may start with *antipasto* (mixed little tastes of seafood, meat and veg) then go on to a *primo piatto* of pasta in the south or risotto in the north, then move to a *secondo piatto* of meat or fish, with *contorni* (vegetables) ordered as an extra. Italians are not big eaters of *dolci* (desserts), except for cakes appropriate to certain feast days, but they might have a piece of fruit or dip some sweet biscuits (*cantucci*) into their coffee. Then they'll return to work, go home, have a walk, and around 9 p.m. they'll tackle *cena* (dinner) with a similar array of courses.

That's the way a meal works if they're eating out, which Italians do a lot, especially if they have visitors (they'd rather entertain at a restaurant than at home) or a big family reunion (a Sunday lunch ritual).

In their homes, they'll eat more simply—maybe just a pasta (Barilla and Buitoni are the biggest selling brands), bread and a salad. In one week, the average family (2.7 people) spends 140,000 lire ($140) on food, consuming 1300 grams of bread, 1000 grams of meat, 670 grams of pasta, 300 grams of fish, 280 grams of cheese, 1.3 litres of milk and 1.1 litres of wine. The Italian diet, with its emphasis on fibre and unsaturated fats, is said to be one of the healthiest in the world.

CONSUMPTION

20
pasta

*t*he last time anybody counted, there were more than 600 types of pasta made in Italy, and some 2,000 names for those 600 varieties. A pragmatist might argue that since pasta is always made simply of flour and water (plus eggs occasionally in the north), there's no good reason for the diversity of shapes. Italians would respond that the shape is a vital contribution to flavour, because whether a pasta is long or short, round or flat, hollow or curly makes all the difference to how a sauce adheres to it and how the air circulates round it in the mouth.

There's a silly myth that spaghetti was brought to Italy from China by Marco Polo in the 13th century. Assuming he even went to China (which is now in doubt), Polo would hardly have been surprised by any edible strings he might have seen there. Flat pasta has been around since the Etruscans. The ancient Romans ate laganum—pastry layered with meat sauce. Noodles seem to have been brought to Sicily by the Arabs around the ninth century, and they then stretched northwards.

Pasta hasn't always been celebrated in Italy the way it is now. In 15th century Florence the rabble-rouser Savanarola delivered this sermon about decadence: 'It's not enough that you eat your pasta fried. No! You think you have to add garlic to it, and when you eat *ravioli*, it's not enough to boil it in a pot and eat it in its own juice, you have to fry it in another pan and cover it with cheese!' A couple of years later Savanarola was roasted alive by an angry crowd. (Mussolini did not learn from this—during World War II he had a tame nutritionist telling Italians that pasta was unhealthy, to reduce consumption when Italy could no longer get enough durum wheat. He fell victim to an angry crowd too.)

It's just as well Savanarola didn't live to see the arrival from the newly discovered Americas of a red fruit they called *pomodoro*, which gave the Italians a whole new sauce. But even as late as the 18th century, pasta was an expensive delicacy for northerners, since the dry form (*pastasciutta*) was only made in the south and had to be transported up the peninsula, while the form made with eggs (*pasta fresca*) stopped at Bologna.

Poor northerners were forced to fill their bellies with rice or polenta (a kind of porridge made with corn meal). Then in 1824 the Agnesi family set up the first mass production pasta factory near Genoa, and brought prices down.

Pasta shapes and accompanying sauces are highly regionalised. The south puts tomato-based sauces on *spaghetti* and *maccheroni* (tubes with sub-species such as *penne* and *rigatoni*). Romans love *gnocchi* (dumplings made with semolina in Rome and with mashed potato and flour elsewhere) and flat noodles called *fettucine*. Tuscans love wide strips called *pappardelle* (with gamey sauces).

The Genoese love *ravioli* (square envelopes stuffed with meat or cheese) and *trenette* (square spaghetti) with pesto sauce (basil and garlic). The Bolognese love *lasagna*, *tortellini* (rings stuffed with meat) and *tagliatelle*, which they serve with an intense meat sauce called a *ragù*. There is no such thing as spaghetti bolognese in Bologna.

Italians were horrified early in 1998 by two rulings that followed from their country's entry into the European Union: first, they must allow the importation of cheap pasta made in other countries with soft wheat, to compete with the Italian durum wheat variety that ensures the pasta will be *al dente* (chewy); second, they must ban the pesticide methyl bromide, because of the damage it does to the ozone layer. Since methyl bromide is mainly used around Genoa to protect sweet basil from insects, there was a fear that the ban would mean the end of pesto sauce. A future of gooey pasta without pesto is close to a definition of hell, but I can't help thinking the Italians will find ways to avoid the crisis.

CONSUMPTION

21
pizza

*t*he presence of 81 discs of dough, perfectly petrified near a brick oven in the ashes of Pompeii, tells us that pizza is at least 2,000 years old, and that the area around Naples can plausibly claim to be its originator. Back then, pizza would not have been smeared with tomato paste (because tomato plants did not arrive in Europe until the 16th century). The covering would have been onions, herbs, cheese and olive oil.

Nowadays the pizza makers of Naples are strict preservers of tradition, abhorring the perversions that have afflicted their creation in other countries (pineapple? rocket? salmon??). The basic *pizza alla napolitana* is a thin crust (of dough which has been kneaded on a marble bench and tossed into the air many times by a highly paid *pizzaiolo*), topped with olive oil, oregano, garlic and chopped tomatoes (preferably the San Marzano variety grown in the Sarno valley), and baked in a wood-fired stone oven.

Pizza Margherita adds

mozzarella cheese (preferably made from the milk of the buffaloes that are farmed between Rome and Naples). The version called *marinara* (so-called because seafarers were supposed to eat it, not because it should contain seafood) has no cheese but can contain olives and chopped anchovies. The only time extravagant fillings are permitted is when the dough is folded over into a *calzone*, which can contain ham, salami, olives, ricotta and even egg.

The best place in the world to try the world's most popular fast food? Two candidates: *Antica Pizzeria Brandi*, which has been baking pizzas since 1800 and claims to have invented the *Margherita* in 1899 in honour of a local Queen (corner of Via Chiaia and Salita Santa Anna di Palazzo near the Royal Palace in central Naples); and *Da Pasqualino*, a big noisy place full of friendly locals (78 Piazza Sanazzaro in the Naples seaside suburb of Mergellina). With pizza you should drink beer, or the south's greatest red wine, Taurasi.

CONSUMPTION

22
restaurants

*t*his is the first rule of eating out in Italy: never go into a place that displays the sign '*Menu Turistico*' or a menu in several languages other than Italian.

There are no more rules. Apart from the most tourist-infested parts of Rome, Venice and Florence, Italy is a country where you can walk into any eating place and expect to find pleasure, because the waiters and the cooks get their job satisfaction that way.

Everyone's pleasure will be enhanced if you've had a look round the local market first (ask directions to *il mercato*), finding out what's plentiful at the moment so you can join the Italians in eating seasonally. You could note down the names of any vegies, mushrooms, and seafood that look interesting in the market, and then ask for them in the place where you're dining. If porcini mushrooms are in season, for example, then the question '*Ha porcini?*' ('Do you have porcini?') will usually provoke a dissertation on how they can be made into a pasta sauce, or grilled whole with garlic, or folded into a risotto. Then you just say '*va bene*' ('Okay') to the option that sounds best.

CONSUMPTION

If the waiter seems friendly, you could try this magic phrase: '*Per piacere, può scegliere per noi dei piatti che sono le specialità dello chef o della località?*' ('Could you choose for us some dishes that are a speciality of the chef or of the locality?') Or you could point to the strangest-sounding thing on the menu.

But perhaps you're not that adventurous. You want a recommendation. The Michelin red guide awards its maximum three-star rating to only three restaurants in Italy: *Dal Pescatore*, just out of the village of Canneto sull'Oglio near Mantua (0376 723 001), specialising in pheasant ravioli, roast goat, and cheese tortelli; *Al Sorriso* in the village of Soriso near Stresa in the far northern lakes district (0322 983 228), specialising in ravioli with goat cheese, and roast pigeon with balsamic vinegar; and *Don Alfonso*, in Sant'Agata sui due Golfi just above Sorrento in the south (0818 780 026), specialising in seafood casserole, lobster with beans and pistachio nuts, and potato cake with mozzarella and basil.

Those places are

THE 100 THINGS...

ristoranti—a word which has connotations of formality and expense, with printed menus and long wine lists. I feel more encouraged when I see a place calling itself a *trattoria*, since it's likely to be casual and family-run. But the naming rules are not rigid: in Venice, a place called *Ristorante Antiche Carampane*, in the relatively tourist-free San Polo area, has an encouraging sign outside which declares '*No pizza, no lasagne, no menu turistico*'. The family member who seats you will ask if you want the antipasto (of course you do) which will be an assortment of various little shellfish that were in the fishmarket this morning, some of them sitting on polenta. Then you'll be asked about pasta, which will be whatever they felt like making today (often spaghetti with *vongole*—little clams—in their shells). Then you'll be shown some fish and asked which one you'd like grilled. It will come with salad and some grilled vegetables (including radicchio, if it's winter). Your choice in wine will be red or white. With coffee you'll get some magnificent home-made pastries. That's how I like to eat in Italy.

The next chapter contains some specific suggestions. Meanwhile, a few **practicalities**: If you know the name of a particular eating place you want to try, it's a good idea to phone and book, to avoid turning up on the one day a week when they close. 'Can I book a table for two this evening at eight

CONSUMPTION

o'clock?' is '*Vorrei riservare un tavolo per due questa sera alle otto?*'

Usually you'll be charged an extra 3,000 lire for '*pane e coperto*' (bread and cover charge), and a service charge of 10 or 15 per cent will be included in the bill. It's customary to leave a couple of thousand lire in change. You must take the receipt (*ricevuta fiscale*) away with you, in case financial inspectors stop you outside the restaurant. They're checking that the place is declaring its earnings for tax purposes. Restaurants are usually honest with the customer but they may not be so scrupulous with the authorities.

CONSUMPTION

23
the list

*t*here's an almost infallible guide to the most interesting restaurants in Italy, but you can't buy it. It has to be given to you.

I first discovered it in a place called Cacciani in the village of Frascati, about an hour away from Rome. Following my usual principle of ordering the least comprehensible dish on the menu, I asked for *rigatoni alla vaccinara*, and found it was pasta with oxtail sauce. As I was smearing up the last of the sauce with my bread, two beaming waiters advanced towards me carrying a terracotta plate on which was a caricature of an ox. It was my reward for choosing the dish of which the chef was proudest.

I learned that Cacciani belonged to a society founded in Milan in 1964 called *L'Unione dei Ristoranti del Buon Ricordo* (the union of restaurants worth remembering). Its members celebrate local traditions in their cooking and resist the pressure to serve spaghetti bolognese to every tourist bus that passes through the neighbourhood. The customer who orders the local speciality gets a souvenir plate depicting it.

Along with my plate at Frascati I received the list

CONSUMPTION

of the 100 other restaurants in the society, and it has guided my travels ever since—to villages and suburbs I would never otherwise have seen and to taste experiences I'd never imagined. I've eaten horse stew in the Dodici Apostoli in Verona, and snail soup in Il Fioretto in Latina, just south of Rome. I've eaten bean soup in Le Padovanelle at the horse trotting track just outside Padua, and squid ink risotto at La Siciliana on the outskirts of industrial Catania. There's even a plate restaurant in a seaside village ten minutes by taxi from Rome airport, so you can check your bags in, pop over to Bastianelli al Molo at Fiumicino for dinner, and prolong the Italian experience till the last minute.

The list keeps changing as restaurants join or leave the society, and the plate specialities change as the chefs get sick of making them. But here is an edited summary, region by region starting in the north-west, of the list as it stands in 1998. The

THE 100 THINGS ...

name of the dish to look for (often in dialect) appears at the end of each entry. Chances are you'll see other dishes on the menu that look interesting too—that's the nature of these restaurants. Your choice comes down to how badly you want the plate (so far, I've collected 26).

☆ **VALLE D'AOSTA**
Hotel Ristorante Casale in the Condemine part of **Saint-Christophe** (near Aosta).
0165/54.12.03. *Pasticcio di fontina su letto di fonduta.*

☆ **PIEMONTE**
Ristorante Antico Buoi Rossi, Via Cavour 32, **Alessandria** (near Turin). 0131/44.50.50. *Coniglio in peperonata.*
Hotel Milano on Lago Maggiore, **Belgirate**. 0322/76.525. *Filetto di salmerino gratinato.*
Ristorante Rosa D'Oro, Viale Medici Del Vascello 2, **Druento** (near Turin). 011/984.66.75. *Pollo alla Marengo.*

☆ **LOMBARDIA**
Taverna Del Colleoni E Dell'Angelo, Piazza Vecchia 7, **Bergamo**. 035/23.25.96. *Stoccafisso mantecato alla moda dell'Angelo.*
Ristorante La Capra, Via Pieve 2, **Cavriana** (near Mantua). 0376/821.01. *Schiena di coniglio con pistacchi e noc.*
Ristorante Tre Pini, Via Morgagni 19, **Milano**. 02/66.80.54.13. *Rustin negà.*

CONSUMPTION

Ristorante Hotel Laurin, Viale Landi 9, **Salo** (near Brescia). 0365/220.22. *Trota in salsa picedo.*
Ristorante Lago Maggiore, Via Carrobbio 19, **Varese.** 0332/23.11.83. *Filetti di persico panati.*

☆ **LIGURIA**

Ristorante Gran Gotto, Viale Brigata Bisagno 69r, **Genova** 010/58.36.44. *Cappellacci di borragine in salsa di pinoli.*
La Fontaine restaurant on the ferry Majestic between Genoa and Palermo, boarding at Via Fieschi 17–17a, **Genoa**. 010/58.93.31. *Zuppa del Commodoro.*
Ristorante Manuelina, Via Roma 278, **Recco** (Italian Riviera near Genoa). 0185/72.07.79. *Cappon magro.*

☆ **VENETO**

Ristorante Hotel Belvedere, Viale Delle Fosse 1, **Bassano Del Grappa.** 0424/52.49.88. *Baccalà alla vicentina.*
Ristorante Tre Panoce, Via Vecchia Trevigiana 50, **Conegliano** (near Treviso). 0438/600.71. *Polastro in tecia col parsemol.*
Ristorante Da Beppe Sello, Via Ronco 68, **Cortina D'Ampezzo.** 0436/32.36. *Carré di cervo saporito.*
Trattoria Dall'Amelia, Via Miranese 113, **Mestre** (on the mainland just across from Venice). 041/91.39.55. *Bigoli in cassopipa.*

Ristorante Antico Brolo, Corso Milano 22, **Padova**. 049/664555. *Testina di vitello all'aceto cotto e cipolla.*
Ristorante Fiaschetteria Toscana, Cannaregio 5719, **Venice**. 041/5285281. *Frittura della Serenissima.*
Ristorante 12 Apostoli, Vicolo Corticella S. Marco 3, **Verona**. 045/59.69.99. *Vitello alla Lessinia.*
Antica Trattoria Tre Visi, Corso Palladio 25, **Vicenza**. 0444/32.48.68. *Porca l'oca in pignatto con funghi.*

☆ TRENTINO ALTO ADIGE
Ristorante Chiesa, Parco San Marco, **Trento**. 0461/23.87.66. *Talleri di Bernardo Clesio.*

☆ EMILIA ROMAGNA
Rosteria Da Luciano, Via Nazario Sauro 19, **Bologna**. 051/23.12.49. *Braciolina antica Bologna.*
Trattoria Da Sandro Al Navile, Via Sostegno 15, **Bologna**. 051/6343100. *Friggione e tortellini.*
Ristorante Gigiole, Piazza Carducci, **Brisighella** (near Ravenna). 0546/812.09. *Costata di castrato al vino rosso con gnocchetti di patate.*
Albergo Ristorante Baia Del Re, Via Vignolese 1684, **Modena**. 059/46.91.35. *Lombata di manzo in salsa d'aceto balsamico.*
Ristorante Parizzi, Via Repubblica 71, **Parma**.

0521/28.59.52. *Tortelli d'erbetta alla parmigiana.*

☆ **TOSCANA**

Ristorante Buca Di S. Francesco, Via S. Francesco I, **Arezzo**. 0575/232.71. *La saporita di Bonconte.*

Ristorante da Delfina, Via della Chiesa 1, **Artimino** (near Florence). 055/871.80.74. *Coniglio con olive e pinoli.*

Ristorante Gennarino, Via Santa Fortunata, **Livorno**. 0586/88.80.93. *Stoccafisso alla Gennarino.*

Ristorante Romano, Via Mazzini 122, **Viareggio**. 0584/313.82. *Zuppa di calamaretti.*

☆ **UMBRIA**

Ristorante Buca Di S. Francesco, Via E. Brizi 1, **Assisi**. 075/812204. *Piccione all'assisana.*

Ristorante Taverna Del Lupo, Via Ansidei 21, **Gubbio**. 075/927.43.68. *Coniglio alla taverniera.*

Ristorante Granaro Del Monte, Hotel Grotta Azzurra, Via Alfieri 12, **Norcia**. 0743/81.65.13. *Filetto del Cavatore.*

Hotel Ristorante Grifone, Via Silvio Pellico 1/5, **Perugia**. 075/583.76.16. *Agnello ai profumi di Colfiorito.*

Hotel Ristorante Le Tre Vaselle, Via G. Garibaldi 48, **Torgiano**. 075/98.80.447. *Millefoglie di vitello al rubesco e anelli di tartufo nero.*

THE 100 THINGS . . .

☆ MARCHE
Ristorante La Pergola, Piazzale Matteotti 45, **Fabriano** (near Ancona). 0732/41.91. *Piccione in fricassea con ravioli tartufati.*

☆ LAZIO
Ristorante Bastianelli al molo, Via Torre Clementina 312, **Fiumicino** (near Rome airport). 06/650.53.58. *Pappardelle con frutti di mare gratinate.*

Ristorante Cacciani, Via Diaz 15, **Frascati**. 06/942.03.78. *Fettuccine alla romana.*

Ristorante Agata E Romeo, Via C. Alberto 45, **Rome**. 06/446.61.15. *Pasta e broccoli con brodo di arzilla.*

Ristorante Alberto Ciarla, Piazza San Cosimato 40, **Rome**. 06/581.86.68. *Baccalà in guazzetto alla romana.*

Trattoria Checchino Dal 1887, Via Monte Testaccio 30, **Rome**. 06/574.63.18, 574.38.16. *Abbacchio alla cacciatora.*

☆ PUGLIA
Ristorante Nuova Vecchia Bari, Via Dante Alighieri 47, **Bari**. 080/521.64.96. *Seppie ripiene al forno.*

Ristorante Piccinni, Via Piccinni 28, **Bari**. 080/521.12.27. *Orecchiette e cime di rapa.*

☆ CAMPANIA
Ristorante 'A Fenestella, Calata del Ponticello a Marechiaro 23, **Naples**. 081/769.00.20. *Linguine alla fenestella.*

☆ BASILICATA
Ristorante La Fattoria, Via Verderuolo Inferiore 13, **Potenza**. 0971/346.80. *Strascinati al ragù di salsiccia.*

☆ SICILIA
Ristorante La Siciliana, Via Marco Polo 52/A, **Catania**. 095/37.64.00. *Calamari ripieni alla griglia.*

Ristorante Hotel Moderno, Via V. Emanuele 63, **Erice**. 0923/86.93.00. *Cuscus con pesce alla trapanese.*

Ristorante La Scuderia, Viale del Fante, **Palermo**. 091/52.03.23. *Merluzzetti alla ghiotta.*

☆ THE ISLAND OF LIPARI
Ristorante Filippino, Piazza Municipio, **Lipari**. 090/981.10.02. *Ravioloni di cernia in salsa paesana.*

☆ SARDEGNA
Ristorante dal Corsaro, Viale Regina Margherita 28, **Cagliari**. 070/66.43.18. *Minestr'e cocciula.*

CONSUMPTION

24
wine

*I*talians like to drink a couple of glasses of wine with meals, but they make no fuss about it. The word *connoisseur* is French. Outside the big cities, you're usually offered *vino della casa* in either *rosso* or *bianco*, and only the more elaborate restaurants have wine lists. You should always try the local stuff. (If you're like me, you will carefully note down the details of the ones you like, only to find they're not available anywhere else in Italy, let alone the world.)

If you're in a place with a wine list, these are some of the more interesting names to look for, moving from north to south ...

Barolo. A big wood-aged red made from Nebbiolo grapes around Alba in the Piemonte region. Exciting modern variations of Barolo include **Barilot** and **Countacc!** (a dialect expression of delight) made by Michele Chiarlo.

Valpolicella. A light lunch red made near Verona. The best forms of it are Jago and Amarone della Valpolicella. Ignore the sweet version called Recioto della Valpolicella.

Pinot Grigio. A crisp white made in the far north, most notably by a company called Jermann.

Torcolato. A luscious dessert wine made by the Maculan company in the Veneto region. Maculan also makes a terrific dry white called Gavi.

Chianti Classico. The best chiantis come from the hills between Florence and Siena, and are marked with a black rooster symbol. They are made to a formula laid down by Baron Bettino Ricasoli early last century, containing mainly Sangioveto grapes with a last minute addition of overripe grapes for richness. Antinori makes a reliable version.

Brunello di Montalcino. Tuscany's most powerful red, with a noticeable vanilla flavour, ideal to drink with beef.

Montepulciano. This is the poor drinker's Brunello, a bit lighter and sharper, but great with pasta.

Tignanello. In recent years some Tuscan winemakers have been using Cabernet Sauvignon to produce big reds that resemble the best of Australia and Bordeaux. The most expensive are Sassicaia and Ornellaia, but Tignanello (made just south of Florence with local Sangioveto grapes as well as Cabernet) offers the same magnificence at a slightly lower price. A similar velvety style is **Carmignano**.

Vin Santo is a kind of sweet heavy sherry made in the Chianti region and pleasant for dipping biscuits at the end of a meal.

Vernaccia. A light white made since medieval times around the Tuscan town of San Gimignano.

Torre di Giano. A crisp white made by the

Torgiano vineyard near Perugia in Umbria. Torgiano is also a name to watch in rich reds.

Taurasi. The great gutsy red from around Naples.

Corvo. A Sicilian red of surprising depth for the price. The name means 'crow', and the best version is Corvo di Salaparuta.

Marsala. A fortified semi-sweet sherry, developed in the west of Sicily in the 18th century by an English entrepreneur hoping to compete with port and madeira.

Grappa. This is a highly alcoholic spirit made by distilling the dregs left after grapes have been pressed for wine. It's unfashionable now in Italy, but if you like heavy liqueurs, you could try refined versions made near Bassano del Grappa by Nardini, Da Ponte or Poli.

Note: Some Italian wines are branded 'DOC' (*Denominazione di Origine Controllata*) which is a guarantee that they are made in the traditional way for their area, and some are marked 'DOCG', which means some of the wine has also been tested by government inspectors. But I've had just as much pleasure with wines labelled '*vino da tavola*'.

CONSUMPTION

25
coffee

*I*talians average four cups of coffee a day, usually taken in their local *caffé* (which functions like a bar or pub in Australia or Britain, since it also serves alcohol and is the social centre of the neighbourhood). They might start the day with a cappuccino. The name derives from the Viennese coffee called the *kapuziner*, which has whipped cream on top (the word describes a brown-robed monk with a white beard). When steam nozzles for frothing milk were developed in 1906, Italians started making their own lighter version of the Vienna special.

If you want more milk and less froth, you ask for a caffé latte. Italians never drink lattes or cappuccinos after midday. They move on to espresso in tiny cups, which can be lengthened to espresso doppio (twice as much caffeine) or caffe lungo (espresso with extra water, sometimes called Caffe Americano).

If you'd like a dash of milk in your espresso, that's a macchiato. (Or if you prefer milk with a dash of coffee, that's a latte macchiato). If you'd like a dash of liqueur, like grappa or brandy, that's a caffe corretto. Decaffeinated coffee is usually called Hag, which is the main brand name, but it's not pleasant.

If you're taking your coffee after dinner, it is customary to have a *digestivo* with it, to settle the stomach. Licorice-flavoured *sambucca* was the fad of the 1970s, but nowadays black bittersweet *amaro* (the best is the Sicilian version called *Amaro Averna*) and yellow soursweet *limoncello* (served ice cold) are more fashionable.

Don't forget: when you leave the caffé, take the receipt with you, and be prepared to show it when requested by a grey-uniformed *guardia di finanza* (an unlikely scenario: the chances are he'll be off having a coffee somewhere).

HABITS

26
siesta

*h*ere's your chance to help save one of Italy's most hallowed institutions. The ancient Romans always took a break from work in the sixth (*sexta*) hour of sunshine and had a rest indoors, because they thought there were dangerous ghosts around at that time of day. From this arose the word and the custom called *siesta*—shutting up shop or office at 1 p.m., eating a leisurely lunch and then taking a little nap (actually called a *pisolino*) before returning to work about 4 p.m. (and plugging on till 7).

The custom fits perfectly with the human body clock, because the brain rhythms slow down about 2 p.m. and don't come back up till 4. So the Anglo

Saxon habit of rushing back from lunch at 2 p.m. is counterproductive, because we make ourselves work at the least efficient time of day.

Sadly, there is now a trend away from siesta in Italy, on the theory that Italians should match the working habits of the barbarians to the north, now that they are part of the European Union. It's up to those of us who visit Italy to make the case for common sense and civilisation—take siesta in our hotels every day, and refuse to patronise any businesses which stay open between 1 p.m. and 4 p.m. (apart from restaurants, of course).

HABITS

27
passegiata

*a*bout 7 p.m. on clement evenings, Italians in cities and villages come out of their homes or offices and walk around. They may do a little window shopping, they may stop for coffee or gelato, and they may kid themselves it's for exercise, but really, the custom called *passegiata* is about Being Seen. It's the opportunity to show off your new clothes, your new haircut, and your new friends, and to watch your neighbours doing the same. It's the time visitors with an interest in the real Italy should be out of their hotels and on the street (even though, as I've explained, a visitor will never be able to achieve *bella figura*).

Young Italians tend to do most of their *passegiata* standing still. They accumulate in a particular spot, lean on their cars or motor scooters, and look at each other. Older people tend to stroll, arm in arm, up and down one favourite block. The activity is also called *lo struscio*, which literally means 'shuffling', but translates better as 'strutting your stuff'.

PASSIONS

28
soccer

*t*he word is *il calcio* (kal-chee-oh, literally 'kick'), which the English call football and the Australians call soccer. The fans are known as *tifosi*—'typhoid victims'. The national team is called the *azzurri* (adze-oori)—'the blues', because of the colour of their shirts.

Soccer in its current form was introduced to Italy late in the 19th century, when English factory owners in Genoa, Turin and Milan set up teams to keep their workers fit. It spread like typhoid, and nowadays, *il calcio* is more powerful than a religion. On any Sunday between September and June (the Italian Cup finals), most people don't go to church, but they tune in to television, or to radio if they're out in a cafe, to learn how their local team is going. Then they spend most of their Mondays conducting post-mortems on the games.

Italy has the most magnificent playing facilities in the world, thanks to a construction program during the 1980s which gave 12 cities palatial stadiums so they could host games for the 1990 World Cup (in which Italy came third).

The victory of the Azzurri in the World Cup in 1982 not only sent Italians into a frenzy—it finally

PASSIONS

united 20 regions which, until then, had barely acknowledged that they were part of one country. So did the shout of agony that came from every Italian throat during the 1994 World Cup when Roberto Baggio failed to kick the goal that might have meant victory over Brazil.

Baggio, a ponytailed Buddhist, was at the time Italy's most admired player (he was bought for $20 million by the businessman Silvio Berlusconi for his AC Milan team). Despite brilliant kicking since then for AC Milan and then for Bologna, Baggio has never recovered from the 1994 embarrassment. When it comes to *calcio*, Italians hold long grudges.

Nowadays the most admired player (and sex symbol) is Alessandro Del Piero, a tiny figure who kicks big goals for the top team Juventus (owned by the Fiat company of Turin, and nicknamed *i bianconeri*, the black and whites, because of their uniforms).

Italians are also interested in Christian Vieri, who grew up in Sydney (his father coached for the Marconi club) and returned to Italy as an adult to become a striker for Juventus. In 1997 they were upset when Vieri was bought by the Spanish team Atletico Madrid, but he

THE 100 THINGS . . .

is still available to play with the Azzurri in World Cup matches every four years.

The words you're most likely to see in headlines in Italy's Monday newspapers are *partita* (match), *vincita* (veen-cheeta, 'win'), *sconfitta* (a defeat), *gol* (a goal), and *totocalcio* (the football pools).

PASSIONS

29
other sports

Sports (apart from exercises called *ginnastica*) are not part of the school curriculum in Italy, but about 16 million Italians—more than a quarter of the population—tell the survey takers that they regularly engage in some form of sport. This is most likely to mean going on skiing holidays or signing up for an exercise program (in designer sportswear) to maintain *bella figura*.

The rest of the country is content just to watch, and after soccer, what they watch is basketball—*pallacanestro* (pulukunestro) in traditional Italian, though most fans use the English word. The top two teams of the late 1990s are both from Bologna, with their names—Teamsystem Fortitudo and Kinder Virtus—revealing the Italian admiration of all things American. There's big money involved: the top two Bologna players, both imports from America, each earn close to $2 million a season, which is more than the Bologna soccer team pays its top player, Roberto Baggio. The total payout to the players in the two Bologna teams is $18 million a season, which is easily covered by ticket sales and sponsorships.

The Italians' love of speed has made them

fascinated by racing in all forms. The San Marino Grand Prix is held in Imola each May, and the Italian Grand Prix is held in Monza each September. Italians are a bit embarrassed by their performance in motor racing in recent years, though Ferrari still builds many of the winning cars. But in cycling, they're on top of the world. Italy builds great bikes (Bianchi and Campagnolo are the names to know) and uses them to effect in the Giro d'Italia, a 25 day cross country race which starts in Nice each May. Gianni Bugno won it in 1992 and 1993, and the hot peddlers of the moment are Marino Picoli and Michele Bartoli. Italy is one of the top motorcycling nations, too, with its champion Giacomo Agostini winning seven consecutive world titles.

The skier most worshipped by Italians is the extraverted Alberto Tomba ('Tomba la bomba'), who won the 1994–95 World Cup. At the other end of the temperature scale, Italians are big on beachgoing but are uninterested in what Australians would think of as surfing. Nevertheless Italy has produced several international swimming champions in recent years, notably Giorgio Lamberti and Emiliano Brembilla (the world number one in 1500 metres freestyle).

PASSIONS

30
sex

*b*ecause most Italians live with their parents until they are married, sex between unmarried people usually means sex in a car (owned by the parents of one of the participants). They are not likely to be well informed about what they are doing, since in many parts of the country there is limited sex education at schools and many parents are reluctant to discuss it.

The pill is used by only 8 per cent of Italian women, and condoms are used even more rarely by men. Since abortion was legalised in the 1980s, it has become a popular form of contraception. There are now about 125,000 abortions a year, which means one abortion for every three live births. Of the women who obtain abortions, 70 per cent are married.

Despite the teachings of the Catholic Church, Italian society is easy-going about sexual display. Pornography is widely available and nudity is frequent on television and in news magazines. It is accepted that married men may have mistresses, although married women are less likely to have lovers, and it is still a serious insult to call an Italian man a *cornuto* (cuckold) or to make the gesture (forefinger and little finger up, other fingers down) indicating his wife is being unfaithful.

Until 1958, brothels were legal in Italy, licensed like bars and subject to regular health checks. Then a Socialist party puritan named Angela Merlin campaigned to have them banned, and prostitutes had to start working the streets.

The curious phenomenon about Italian streetwalkers is that many of them are actually men—transsexuals and transvestites, who apparently cater to a theory that men are not being unfaithful to their wives if they have sex with someone who is not female. *I trans* are so popular that they charge more than *vere puttane* (genuine hookers), although in recent years the Italian-born transsexuals have been undercut by transsexuals arriving from Brazil (known as *i viados*), and street fights have erupted between national *tran* teams.

Other terms to know are: *mi piaci* (I fancy you), *una scopata* (a fuck), *una sveltina* (a quickie), *cazzo* (cock), *fica* (cunt, as opposed to *fico*, a fig), *profilattico* (a condom).

ICONS

31
cars

a beautifully designed and frequently polished car is an important way to demonstrate *bella figura*, so Italy has the second highest rate of car ownership in the world, after the United States. (America has 564 cars per 1,000 citizens, Italy has 524 and Australia comes third with 499.) Although the rich like to show off with Mercedes and Aston-Martins, the mass of Italians are intensely loyal to their own car company, Fiat.

Two thirds of the cars driven in Italy are made by Fiat (or a subsidiary such as Lancia, Ferrari, Alfa-Romeo or Autobianchi) and that would be the case even if there weren't tough import restrictions on Japanese cars, because Fiat's production standards are so high.

It employs designers who have become legendary around the world, notably **Sergio Pininfarina**, who created the bodies of most classic Ferraris and Lancias inside Italy, as well as assorted Peugeots,

THE 100 THINGS ...

Cadillacs and Rolls Royces outside the country; and **Giorgio Giugiaro** (jor-joe jew-jar-oh), who moved on from the Fiat Uno, the Alfa Sud and assorted Maseratis to design the VW Golf and the Korean Hyundai. (In the early 1980s, the Voiello pasta company of Naples commisioned Giugiaro to design a new pasta shape, and he came up with a streamlined model he called the Marille, containing two tubes and a curving tail. It looked like a roller coaster ride or possibly a handwritten 'g', which happens to be the most frequent letter in its designer's name.)

The Italians' driving style, like their way of dealing with bureaucracy, is best described as flexible. They ride very close on each other's tails, and seem to regard red lights, lane markings and short one-way streets as optional. They have no enthusiasm for seat belts or for reducing their use of polluting types of petrol. They have one of Europe's worst records for minor accidents (*incidente*), but their rate of deaths by car accident is in the middle—14 per 100,000 people each year, compared with 10 in Australia, 15 in the US, and 30 in South Korea.

ICONS

32
design

*W*hether or not Leonardo da Vinci actually invented the bicycle, there's no doubt Italians have long excelled at creating objects that are both practical and beautiful. This skill turned into a world fad in the 1970s, after an exhibition at New York's Museum of Modern Art, called 'Italy: The New Domestic Landscape', showed how products as ordinary as coffee pots and telephones could become sculptures. Since most of the elegant objects on display at that exhibition were designed in small studios in Milan, that city became the hot place to study and to shop.

During the 1980s, Milan's Memphis studio was the world's most influential furniture designer. Nowadays, even Italian firms that manufacture far from Milan pretend to be Milanese by operating their main showrooms there.

The key names to know in Italian design are: **Alessi**, for whom Michael Graves designed a legendary kettle and

THE 100 THINGS ...

Ettore Sottsass designed sleek cutlery (after earlier making his name with a portable typewriter for Olivetti and a vast array of objects for Memphis); **Artemide,** who make furniture (including the Selene stackable plastic chair designed by **Vico Magistretti**) and lamps that combine metal and glass; **Brionvega,** who make radios and TV sets; **Piero Fornasetti,** who illustrated everything from ties to wastepaper baskets; **Michele De Lucchi,** who creates lights and shop interiors; **Olivetti,** who set world standards for sleek office equipment; **Zonatta,** who make furniture, including a classic folding table designed by **Achille Castiglione**. And that's not even mentioning the jewellery developments of Beltrami, Bulgari, Buccellati and UNO-AR.

While all this does wonders for Italy's international image and export figures, Milan's designer objects have little impact on everyday life in their homeland. They are more likely to be seen in New York apartments or Sydney terraces than in the average Italian home.

ICONS

33
fashion

though they have a mysterious affection for the tweedy English look, the Italians are obsessed with 'Made in Italy'. In the past two decades the world has joined them, letting Milan take over from Paris as the arbiter of international dress sense.

The image of Italian dominance has been boosted by sensational publicity surrounding the designers themselves—the 1995 shooting of Maurizio Gucci, for which his ex-wife and her psychic were charged in 1997, and the 1997 shooting of Gianni Versace, apparently by a gay American serial killer (though Italian *dietrologia* linked it with Versace's refusal to meet the demands of the Mafia).

Then, as part of the Clean Hands investigation of the mid 1990s, four of Italy's top fashion names—Giorgio Armani, Krizia, Gianfranco Ferre and Santo Versace (brother of Gianni)—were charged with bribing tax inspectors to avoid tax audits. They admitted paying the bribes, but their defence was that this was the

The handbag's Gucci; The shoes are Gucci; The handcuffs... Gucci

normal way of doing business in Italy at the time.
The names to know in Italian fashion are:

☆ **ARMANI.** Giorgio Armani initially worked as a designer for Nino Cerrutti, a textile maker, then set up a freelance studio in 1970, had a hit with serious menswear, and became famous in the early 1980s for introducing 'dress for success' women's suits that managed also to be beautiful.

☆ **BENETTON.** Founded in the 1970s by five brothers and sisters in Treviso, near Venice, it is now the world's biggest buyer of wool, with 4,000 franchised shops around the world selling bright youthful clothes. Luciano Bennetton is known in Italy for his successful Formula One car racing team, and internationally for his surprising magazine advertisements which confront issues such as racism and AIDS.

☆ **FERRÉ.** Gianfranco Ferré produced his first line of ready-to-wear clothes for women in 1978, but moved up to high fashion in the mid 1980s, and was appointed chief designer for the French house of Dior in 1989.

☆ **GUCCI.** Founded as a small leathergoods shop in Florence in 1920 by Guccio Gucci, a former waiter, it spread round the world in the 1950s, then made the mistake of going mass-market. In the late 1980s, after declining sales and battles within the family, Gucci reduced its range from 20,000 products to 5,000 products (mainly shoes, handbags and suitcases) and recovered some of its elite image. It is now owned by the Arab company Investcorp.

☆ **VALENTINO.** His full name is Valentino Garavani, his logo is a V, and he's from Voghera, north of Milan, though his first fashion show was in Florence in 1962, after an apprenticeship with Paris clothes makers. His dresses were popularised by Jacqueline Onassis and Elizabeth Taylor, but he has launched a younger line called Oliver, named after his dog.

☆ **VERSACE.** First noticed as an outrageous dress designer with a fetish for safety pins in the late 1970s, Versace turned his line into a $2 billion a year industry. Since his death, his sister Donatella is keeping up the business.

☆ **ZEGNA.** Now run by Ermenegildo, the grandson of the original suitmaker, this company has a $2 billion annual turnover making 30 per cent of the world's upmarket wool suits for men.

☆ **GFT.** Most fashion fans outside Italy have never heard of Gruppo Finanzario Tessile, run by the Rivetti family of Turin, but without it, most other Italian fashion companies could not operate. It's a textile maker employing 7,000 people to make five million garments a year for the likes of Armani and Ungaro.

HISTORY

34
how it started

*t*hree thousand years ago the Greeks colonised the toe of the boot we now call Italy, while the Etruscans emerged as the dominant tribe around the ankle, forming a loose alliance of city states between the Tiber and the Arno rivers. The Etruscans mined the iron in the area and traded it for art objects brought by Phoenicians from the east and Greeks from the south.

The year 753 BC is the legendary date for the founding of the city of Rome, supposedly by the twins Romulus and Remus, who were brought up from infancy by a she-wolf. The first inhabitants were mainly members of the Latin and Sabine tribes, who were ruled by the Etruscans till 509 BC, when the top families overthrew the Etruscan King Tarquin and declared Rome a republic.

The Romans then set about conquering all the land around them, driving out the Etruscans and the Greeks, and ending up with control of the peninsula by the second century BC. They had a minor setback when Hannibal, a general from Carthage in northern Africa (now Tunisia) brought an army across the Alps on elephants and got as far as Rome in 217 BC. But after three Punic Wars,

HISTORY

Rome destroyed Carthage, then took over Sicily, Greece, Spain and most of the Mediterranean.

All this fighting gave tremendous power to the army, and in 80 BC, General Sulla staged a military coup and wiped out most of the Senate. He was followed by Pompey, who in turn was overthrown by Julius Caesar (who had been the hero of Rome's conquest of Gaul). Caesar took the title Dictator For Life, but this did not turn out to be a long time, since he was assassinated in 44 BC by a group of senators led by his adopted son Brutus.

Caesar's nephew Octavius seized power and became the first Roman emperor, with the title Augustus Caesar. He began a program of road and temple building and of encouraging the arts which lasted for 200 years after his death. But not every emperor was as visionary as Augustus—Tiberius was a murderer, Caligula was a loony, Claudius was a weakling, and Nero was a sadist who proved so destructive that the Senate ordered him flogged to death.

By 200 AD, the Roman empire was weakening, under attack from Germanic tribes from the north. In 313, the emperor Constantine moved the capital from Rome to Byzantium. In 410, Rome was invaded by the Visigoths, then the Vandals.

HISTORY
35
the middle ages

When the Roman Empire collapsed under barbarian invasions in the fifth century, there was only the Christian church to hold Italian culture together (and to accumulate relics and treasures from pilgrims). By the sixth century, Rome's population had shrunk to a few thousand, and the self-proclaimed kings of Italy (actually Ostrogoths) lived in Ravenna.

In 536, the Emperor Justinian, who ran what was left of the eastern Roman empire from Constantinople, invaded Italy (with mostly Greek-speaking troops) and defeated the Goths, placing his own representatives in charge of key cities. This introduced a short period of Byzantine influence on Italian art, but in 568, a German tribe called the Lombards overran northern Italy. The Popes asked a tribe called the Franks to protect the area round Rome from the Lombards. Meanwhile, Muslims from Tunisia were moving into Sicily and parts of the south.

Some order came out of the anarchy in the tenth century when a German invader named Otto the Great took over most of Italy and had himself crowned Holy Roman Emperor. He provided

HISTORY

enough stability in the area north of Rome for city states (known as *communi*) such as Milan, Pisa, Venice and Florence to begin growing in power (and fighting each other), under the rule of rich trading families. The south, meanwhile, fell to the Normans, who mingled their own culture with that of the Arabs. Then came the marriage of a Norman princess to a German prince named Frederick, enabling him to become king of Sicily in 1198 and Holy Roman Emperor in 1220.

But the issue of papal power versus imperial power divided Italians. The pro-Pope faction was called the Guelphs (colour: white; battlements: square) and the pro-emperor faction was called the Ghibellines (colour: black; battlements: v-shaped). They engaged in skirmishes for most of the 13th century. Siena, for example, was a Ghibelline town and in 1260 it conquered Florence, which was Guelph.

When the church whipped up European leaders to start the crusades, Venice and Pisa made a fortune providing boats, and the city states continued to profit from the opening up of trade routes around the Mediterranean and into the east. By the start of the 14th century, most of Italy was doing extremely well. It could hardly be called The Dark Ages any longer.

HISTORY

36
the renaissance

*t*he French language has given us the word for the artistic, literary and scientific blossoming that took place in the 14th century. But we should call it the *rinascimento*, since it happened in Italy. Perhaps the French got a say in it because, at the time it was starting, the Pope was living in Avignon as a puppet of the king of France.

The *rinascimento* happened because rich people have to spend their money on something. By the 14th century, the peninsula called Italy contained four powerful nations: Venice, an exotic trading port and a republic which spread its control east to the Greek islands and west to Brescia; Florence, big in banking and the wool trade, with a seaport at Pisa; Milan, big in arms, textiles, and agriculture; and the kingdom of Naples, which controlled the south, including Sicily. There were also smaller principalities including Ferrara, Genoa, Siena, Lucca, Mantua and Savoy-Piedmont (in the northwest, near France), as well as the Papal states around Rome.

The merchant families who controlled the city-states wanted to boost their egos by encouraging local artists. In Florence, the Medici dynasty,

HISTORY

founded by the banker Giovanni de Medici, reached its highest point with Lorenzo the Magnificent, who ruled from 1469 to 1492 and was the patron of Michelangelo. Lorenzo's son Giovanni became Pope in 1523, thus uniting Florence with the Papal states.

In Milan, the Sforza dynasty reached its highest point with Ludovico, who ruled from 1480 to 1499 and was the patron of Leonardo da Vinci. And in Ferrara (near Bologna) the d'Este family encouraged the paintings of Titian and Bellini and the writings of Petrarch (who created a new form of sonnet), Tasso (who wrote the epic poem *Jerusalem Delivered*) and Ariosto (who wrote an epic masterpiece called *Orlando Furioso*). Social note: Alfonso d'Este married Lucrezia Borgia (her first two husbands having died under suspicious circumstances).

It was too good to last. At the end of the 15th century, the Duke of Milan invited the king of France to join him in trying to take control of Naples. This upset the Spanish, who moved in and took control of Naples for themselves, and over the ensuing years, Charles V of Spain became Holy Roman Emperor and ruler of most of Italy. With him came the Inquisition, which enforced a strict form of Catholicism designed to prevent the kind of Christian breakaways that were happening elsewhere in Europe. Venice, Lucca and Florence were the only significant city states which retained their independence.

From 1600, Italy went into an economic decline,

THE 100 THINGS . . .

though art and science still flourished. The late 17th century saw a Naples-based peasants' revolt against Spanish rule, but it was brutally suppressed. In the early 18th century, the Hapsburgs of Austria took control of Milan and much of Italy's north and of the kingdom of Naples, which then was put into the hands of a Spanish branch of the Bourbon family. The weakness and inefficiency of most of the rulers made Italy wide open for conquest by a reincarnation of Julius Caesar, and a Corsican general named Napoleon Bonaparte thought he was just the man for the job.

HISTORY

37
one nation

*h*ere's why so many streets in Italy are called Mazzini, Garibaldi or Cavour, and why a sauce is called Marengo ...

Napoleon swept down from France in 1796 and by 1801 had come close to unifying Italy for the first time since the Roman empire. His triumph against the Austrians at the battle of Marengo is celebrated in the Piedmont region these days with a sauce for veal or chicken that contains tomatoes, garlic, white wine, cognac and fried eggs—as served to Napoleon after the decisive battle.

Napoleon crowned himself King of Italy, put various relatives in charge of its regions, tried to reorganise the legal system and carted thousands of artworks off to the Louvre. When he was overthrown by armies from the rest of Europe in 1814, the Congress of Vienna divided Italy into a bunch of principalities again. But the Italians had developed a taste for unity, and a revolutionary movement began to grow. It came to be known as the *Risorgimento*.

The intellectual leader of the push to weld the various countries within Italy into one republic was Giuseppe Mazzini, who formed the Young Italy movement and managed to foment uprisings in the streets of most of the major cities in 1848. Intervention by the European powers stopped that revolution, and the liberationists' strategy changed from building a republic to trying to unify the country under the King of Piedmont, Vittorio Emanuele II.

The diplomacy necessary to bring this about was done by Count Camillo di Cavour, the chief minister of Piedmont, and most of the fighting was organised by a former sailor named Giuseppe Garibaldi. Cavour persuaded the French to help him defeat the Austrians who controlled much of the north, while Garibaldi tackled the south. In 1859 Garibaldi, with a thousand supporters wearing red shirts, landed in Sicily and rallied the locals to help him overthrow the authorities there, moving up to Naples and claiming it for King Victor Emanuel in 1860. Rome fell to the forces of Piedmont in 1870.

Although now unified under one government, Italy remained factionalised and temperamental. Its government took it into World War I on the Allies' side in hopes of gaining territory around Trieste, but it emerged from the war impoverished. Once again it was wide open for the attentions of a leader who fancied himself as the reincarnation of Julius Caesar.

HISTORY

38
Mussolini

*i*n the chaos that followed World War I, a nationalist movement called Fascism was starting to look attractive to many Italians. Its inventor was Benito Mussolini, who had been editor of a socialist newspaper called *Avanti*, and who recruited a bunch of young war veterans in the north of Italy and dressed them in black shirts to fight the rise of communism. Backed by small shopkeepers and big industrialists, Mussolini and his *Fascisti* (from the word *fasci*, which were the bundles of rods that symbolised authority in ancient Rome) marched on Rome from Milan in 1922. Nervous King Vittorio Emanuele III decided resistance was futile, and appointed Mussolini prime minister.

He assumed dictatorial powers two years later, imprisoned and killed political opponents, started a series of monumental building projects and state-controlled business ventures, suppressed crime and dissent, made an agreement with the Vatican that gave it the status of an independent country within Italy, colonised Abyssinia and Albania, and made an alliance with Hitler that took a reluctant populace into World War II.

In 1943, as the Allies were invading Sicily, Mussolini was arrested by his own governing council and imprisoned in a ski hotel in the Abruzzo mountains. The government then u-turned and declared itself to be on the side of the Allies, but Mussolini wasn't finished yet. He was rescued by the Germans and made ruler of the northern quarter of Italy, which was called 'the Italian social republic', and based in Salò, Lombardy.

The northern Italians proved highly efficient as resistance fighters against Mussolini and the Germans, and in 1945 the partisans captured him and his mistress and hung their bullet-riddled bodies upside down from the roof of a petrol station in Milan.

With the war over, Italians voted to abolish the monarchy and finally got the republic they'd started fighting for 100 years earlier.

HISTORY

39
world domination

*I*taly—or, more precisely, the part of Italy that lies north of Rome—started to boom in the 1950s, and the boom has never stopped. Individual energy and creativity transcended the chaotic political system and massively boosted the wealth of the average Italian. One statistic demonstrates it: in 1948, there were 150,000 cars on the road in Italy; in 1996, there were 26 million.

Since the collapse of the Roman empire, Italy has been an utter failure at military conquest. But after World War II the Italians proceeded to take over the Western world by more subtle means. They colonised us through our eyes and through our stomachs. What's the most fashionable food in America, Britain and Australia? Pasta. What's the most fashionable adult drink? Cappuccino. What names do we respect at the movies? De Niro, Di-Caprio, Scorsese, Pacino, Fellini, Tarantino, Antonioni, Travolta, DeVito,

Rossellini, Stallone. Okay, maybe not Stallone. How do we hope to dress? Like someone who frequents the fashion houses of Milan. What kind of car defines sleekness and elegance? Fiat, Ferrari, Maserati, Lamborghini, and Alfa-Romeo. Which nation's designers made an art form out of everyday objects such as kettles, typewriters and cheese graters? Italy's. What's the lifestyle to which we all aspire? Mediterranean.

La dolce vita has been Italy's most successful export.

MONEY

40
the economy

*I*taly has the fastest growing economy in Europe, and ranks seventh among the world's industrialised nations—and that's not even including all the undeclared black market activity that goes on. It has an inflation rate of about three per cent and an unemployment rate of about 12 per cent (though much worse in the south than in the north). Since World War II, the economy has changed from mainly agricultural to mainly industrial, and now the service industry is the fastest growing sector. Italy earns its living these days by selling to the world machinery, steel, chemicals, processed food, cars, clothes, shoes, ceramics and tourism. It still has to import 75 per cent of its raw materials and its energy needs.

In the early 1990s, a massive budget deficit, partly caused by the high cost of maintaining the system of kickbacks to political parties, put Italy at risk of not being allowed to join the European Monetary

Union. Its public debt was 122 per cent of its Gross Domestic Product—twice the level which is supposed to apply to signatories of Europe's Maastricht treaty. But luckily, most of the government's debt is to its own citizens: It has regularly raised money by selling high interest bonds, called BOT, which became a popular method of saving for Italians.

In 1998, Italy just squeaked into the Monetary Union by raising some taxes, trimming its deficit, scaling back its elaborate pension system, lowering interest rates and cutting its public debt. (Private debt was always low—Italians are the world's most cautious users of credit cards, and they prefer to save up for their homes rather than get mortgages.)

Most Italian economists think the government will be unable to maintain cost-cutting to reach the standards of other European countries, because Italians will not tolerate a drop in their standard of living. But they don't see this as a problem. As Paolo Leon, an economist at the University of Rome, said: 'We have a moral obligation to steadily reduce our public debt. But there is nothing about that on paper. If there is a recession, then we will behave as typical Italians—we will not respect the Maastricht parameters. What can they do? We are in, and they cannot kick us out.'

MONEY

41
big business

*t*he biggest business in Italy is the government. It owns the nation's largest company—Istituto per la Ricostruzione Industriale (Institute for Industrial Reconstruction), better known as IRI, which was set up by Mussolini in 1933, and expanded by Christian Democrat administrations after World War II—an ironic piece of socialism for a party set up to combat communism.

IRI dominates steel production, engineering, banking, telecommunications (owning Stet, the phone company), aviation (Alitalia), broadcasting (the RAI networks), and tourism (the CIT agency). IRI underwent massive efficiency reforms in the 1980s (when it was headed by Romano Prodi, now Italy's prime minister), and in 1997 it declared a profit of $5.2 billion.

Another government-owned company, ENI (Ente Nazionale per Idrocarboni) controls the expressways, the AGIP petrol stations, and a variety of chemical businesses. The government-owned shipbuilding company, Fincantieri, makes 40 per cent of the world's cruise ships, as well as military ships, car ferries and diesel engines, in a gigantic shipyard north of Venice.

THE 100 THINGS ...

During the 1990s the government has been selling off chunks of its enterprises. The president of IRI, Gian Maria Gros-Pietro, announced in 1998 that the privatisation program would earn $20 billion between 1998 and 2000 (a useful way around the public debt problem), but that the government would aim to retain a small interest in most of the businesses it was selling.

The government's major competitor is the Agnelli family, which controls Fiat, Italy's largest private business. But don't just think cars when you hear that name. Fiat makes aircraft engines, helicopters, trains, buses, weapons, chemicals and telecommunications equipment, and, in the course of all that, places a seventh of all the advertising in the Italian media. Fiat employs 250,000 people with another two million dependent on it in associated industries.

The Agnelli holding company, IFI, also controls banks, insurance companies, the department store chain Rinascente, and the daily newspapers *La Stampa* and *Corriere della Sera*. In 1997, IFI declared a profit of $470 million—a rise of five per cent on the previous year.

MONEY

42
Berlusconi

*h*e may not be Italy's richest businessman (that title goes to Gianni Agnelli, boss of Fiat), but Silvio Berlusconi is certainly the most powerful. These are edited highlights of what he controls (with total assets of more than $5 billion): Fininvest, Italy's second largest private firm, which owns the country's three commercial television networks and the biggest video film library outside Hollywood; the supermarket chain Standa and the retail chain Euromercato; Edilnord, one of Italy's biggest real estate empires and a builder of holiday resorts; the publishing house Mondadori, which produces Italy's best-selling magazine *TV Sorrisi e Canzoni* (TV Smiles and Songs); the giant life insurance company Mediolanum; and the soccer team AC Milan. Not bad for a former cruise ship entertainer who made his first million building blocks of flats on the outskirts of Milan.

In 1993, Berlusconi decided all this wasn't enough—he wanted to be prime minister too. He created a political party called *Forza Italia* ('Go Italy!', the cry from the stands at international soccer matches) and personally selected a bunch of candidates (mostly executives from his companies) on their ability to sell themselves on television. Forza Italia didn't seem to stand for anything except 'making Italy great again' and anti-communism (at a time when communism had already self-destructed), but Italians were so disgusted with the corrupt older parties that they gave it the highest share of the vote. Berlusconi pulled together a coalition with other conservative groups (including the neo-Fascists) and became prime minister in May 1994.

But then his star began to fall. The Clean Hands investigators announced he was under investigation for bribing tax officials, falsifying accounts, and bribing judges to get favourable verdicts in cases involving his companies. His government tried to limit the power of magistrates to detain suspects in Clean Hands investigations, and got widely condemned.

Then one of the coalition partners, the Northern League, withdrew from the government, forcing Berlusconi to resign as prime minister. Forza Italia's vote dropped in the 1996 elections, and soon afterwards Berlusconi was sentenced to 16 months jail for fraud (though the appeal process will take years). Now he leads the opposition parties in the Italian parliament, and does not shrink from using his votes to advance his own business interests.

In 1998, Berlusconi, now in his mid 60s, tried to sell a stake in his TV company Mediaset to Rupert Murdoch, but said the offer of $3.3 billion was not enough. This suggested he might be trying to cash up and ease into retirement—perhaps to concentrate on improving his football team, AC Milan, whose decline in the mid 1990s paralleled his own.

MONEY

43
work

*W*orking conditions in Italy fit with the national philosophy that life is to be enjoyed, not suffered. Most workers get five or six weeks annual holiday, as well as 10 public holidays each year. Working hours have traditionally been 9 a.m. to 1 p.m. and 3 p.m. to 7 p.m., five days a week, but recently there's been a shift towards 9 to 5, as some businesses try to match the working hours of the northern European barbarians.

At the beginning of December most workers get an extra month's salary called a *tredicesima* ('thirteenth'). The *tredicesima* was introduced in the 1960s as a bonus to reward productivity, but now it is supplied automatically, even to people on pensions.

There are three main categories of workers, and each group spends a great deal of time complaining about the other two. First there are the *statali*, the public servants (who represent nearly 40 per cent of the workforce). Many of them work from 8 a.m. to 2 p.m., which means they can take second jobs in the evenings. The state gives them a generous pension scheme (they can retire after 20 years service), subsidised holiday camps, low interest mortgages, health insurance, and discounts on public transport. They are the most envied workers in the country, and competition for public service jobs is fierce. The *statali* tend to vote for the National Alliance (the neo-fascists), which accounts for that party's resistance to public service reform even though it is supposed to be pro-capitalist.

Then there are the *autonomi*, the self-employed, the small business people, who are stereotyped as tax dodgers and who complain about the laziness of the *statali* and the failure of the state to encourage individual enterprise. They tend to vote for the Northern League or Forza Italia.

Third and most long-suffering of the groups are the *dipendenti*, salaried workers in private enterprise whose taxes are deducted from their wages (so they can't dodge) and who miss out on the generous pension schemes of the *statali*. They tend to be active in unions and to vote for the Democratic Party of the Left.

MONEY

44
status

*l*ike most Westerners, Italians indulge in a fair bit of snobbery based on wealth, but even if you're not rich, you can enhance your *bella figura* with a title. The government can make you either a *Commendatore* or a *Cavaliere* for services to society or business, but the unofficial titles are just as important. Being an intellectual is much admired, and if you have a university degree related to the humanities, or if you act as if you do, you are likely to be addressed as *dottore*. If you are in a technical profession, you'll be addressed as *ingegnere*, or as *avvocato* if you work in the law, *architetto* if you design buildings, *onorevole* if you're a member of parliament, *padrone* if you run a small business (like a restaurant), and *ragioniere* (accountant) if you do bookkeeping. If you have a higher degree or some reputation in a field, you'll be known as *professore* or *maestro*. You may score a '*grazie, professore*' if you look distinguished and leave a big tip.

The use of English can

add value to a title. It's flattering to be called *un manager, un executive, un VIP* or *un topmodel*.

The Italians have fun with the titles game, applying them as nicknames to their public figures. Thus the boss of Fiat, Gianni Agnelli, is always known as *l'Avvocato*; Carlo de Benedetti, the boss of Olivetti, is known as *l'Ingegnere*; and Silvio Berlusconi, boss of commercial TV, is known as *Sua Emittenza* (a pun on the religious title 'his eminence', referring to the 'emitting' of broadcasts).

The fact that Raul Gardini, the boss of the chemical company Montedison, did not have a university degree was no deterrent to the title-givers. He was known as *Il Contadino* ('the peasant'). He bore it proudly, especially when he led an Italian attempt to win the America's Cup in yachting, but it was no protection when he was accused, as part of the Clean Hands investigation, of creating a huge slush fund to bribe politicians. In 1993, at the age of 60, *Il Contadino* blew his brains out.

PIONEERS

45 women

*P*olitically, feminists have had huge victories in Italy since they became active in the late 1960s. Divorce was legalised in 1974, abortion was legalised in 1981, and in 1988, the Constitutional Court ruled that only the woman has any rights in deciding whether an abortion should take place.

Women now receive 53 per cent of the university degrees (45 per cent of medical degrees, and 56 per cent of science degrees). Italian women usually keep their single names after they marry for the purposes of official documents.

But still, more than 90 per cent of management positions in government and business are held by men. Only 33 per cent of women are in the full-time workforce in the north of Italy (and 25 per cent in the south)—a much lower female participation rate than in most Western countries (in Australia, 54 per cent of women are in the workforce).

In the home, feminism has a long way to go. Italian men still expect that women will do all the child rearing and nearly all the housework. One survey in the early 1990s showed that in the average household, the woman does 36 hours housework a week to the man's 5.5 hours. When the woman has a full time job, the man's share rises to 6 hours.

46
gays

*I*talian men are more physically demonstrative with each other than men in Anglo countries, and homosexuality is not illegal in Italy, but it is condemned by the Church and subject to some social disapproval. Gay politicians do not tend to go public about their preferences. Homosexuality is a reason for a young man to be exempted from compulsory military service, and a law passed in 1990 forbids gays from donating blood.

The activist group is called ARCI-Gay, which has about 15,000 members. It is based in Bologna, because that city has a history of tolerance of diversity, even though the city with the largest gay population is Milan.

In the mid 1990s ARCI-Gay became concerned at the failure of authorities to do anything about what appeared to be a serial killer of gay men operating in Rome. The media only took up the issue when a senior Vatican official, Enrico Sini Luci, was found in his apartment looking as if his head had been bashed in after rough sex. He turned out to be the 19th gay man murdered in a similar way in Rome since 1990. The President of ARCI-gay, Franco Grillini, said there was 'a national emergency' of 'social violence generated by homophobia'. He called on the Vatican to condemn violence against homosexuals. The Vatican did not respond. The killer is still uncaught.

RITUALS

47 marriage

*a*s in other Western countries, Italy's marriage rate is dropping and its divorce rate is rising, but both trends are happening very slowly. There are now 292,600 weddings a year (compared with 440,000 in 1947), with some 82 per cent of them in a Catholic church. The guests throw rice (never confetti, which is the Italian word for the sugar-coated almonds given to the wedding guests by the happy couple).

There are 24,000 divorces a year and 48,000 formal separations (for those who do not wish to offend the Church). About ten per cent of marriages fail, but four out of five divorced Italians remarry. The conventional wisdom is that the marriages most likely to fail are those between people from different regions, because their tastes in food are likely to be incompatible.

RITUALS

48
the home

Some 65 per cent of Italians own their own homes (one of the highest rates of ownership in the world, and not far behind Australia's), while 14 per cent have a second home for weekends. Less than 20 per cent have mortgages—the home would more likely have been bought by family members pooling their savings and paying cash. And once they're in, they'll stay for life.

The average home these days (more likely a two bedroom apartment in a renovated old building than a free-standing house) contains 2.8 people, compared with 3.9 in the 1950s. That's a result of the lower birth rate and the rise in personal wealth.

It is likely to have wooden floors if it's in the north or tile floors if it's in the south, because Italians think the Anglo habit of laying wall to wall carpet is unhealthy. In the winter they'll partly cover their floor with a couple of exotic rugs (Italy is the world's

THE 100 THINGS ...

biggest importer, per capita, of Turkish and Persian rugs).

Because Italians are obsessed with security, the house or apartment complex will have an elaborate locking system on both windows and doors, a remote-controlled front door, and surveillance cameras in wealthier areas. And because they love gadgets, the bathroom will probably have complicated taps and a toilet flushing mechanism that's hard to find.

RITUALS

49
animals

*M*ost Italians tend not to have family pets, because they would rather spend their money on spoiling the children, and they're sure animals would bring germs into the house. For older couples without children, small dogs are fashionable, and are sometimes brought into restaurants. People with large houses may obtain an Alsatian or a Doberman as part of the security system, allowing the dogs to stay outside and keep the neighbours awake by barking.

Cats are rarely kept as pets. They run wild all over Italian cities, fed on leftovers by little old ladies. In Rome there is a law forbidding the killing of stray cats or even driving them away from where they were born.

Italians are uninterested in zoos, and if you want an insight into their indifference to animals, visit the Giardino Zoologico in the north of Rome's Borghese Gardens. You'll find a few antelopes and wolves, plenty of stray cats and very few people.

RITUALS

50
religion

*t*he ancient Romans borrowed the religion of the ancient Greeks but changed the names of the deities. The gist of it (as explained by Ovid and as portrayed on a million statues throughout Italy) was that the universe was born when Uranus (the heavens) and Gaea (the earth) emerged from Chaos and mated (the big bang?). Gaea produced 12 giants called Titans and 12 monsters. The youngest Titan, Saturn, overthrew his father and became king of the universe. Then he married his sister Rhea and produced six children, but decided to eat them in case they did to him what he had done to his own dad.

Rhea fed Saturn a stone instead of the sixth child, Jupiter, and when he grew up, Jupiter overthrew Saturn and released his brothers and sisters from his father's stomach. Then he set up a kingdom on Mount Olympus in Greece and ruled the universe with a cabinet of 13 other deities, each with particular ministerial responsibilities: Jupiter's wife Juno (child-bearing); Bacchus (wine and festivity); Ceres (harvest); Diana (hunting); Mars (war); Mercury (messages); Minerva (wisdom); Neptune (sea); Phoebus (light and music); Pluto (the

RITUALS

underworld); Venus (love and beauty); Vesta (the home); Vulcan (fire).

That was the Italian religious system when followers of a Jew named Jesus, who had been executed in Jerusalem, started arriving in Rome in the middle of the first century. Since they believed in only one deity, they were not well received—the emperor Nero tried to blame them for a fire which he'd probably started himself, and they were subjected to regular persecution. But the Romans allowed them to build vast underground tunnels called catacombs on the edge of the city, in order to bury their dead (since the Romans used cremation). In the year 315, the emperor Constantine had a vision of a cross in the sky, and declared Christianity to be the official religion of the (by now somewhat fragmented) Roman empire.

As Rome fell victim to various barbarian invasions, the Church was the only force for continuity in Italian culture. The Popes accumulated wealth from pilgrims heading for Rome to see holy relics, and survived by doing deals with European tribal leaders.

From the 15th century, various factions of Christianity elsewhere in Europe rejected the authority of the Pope and split from the Church based in Rome, which came to be known as the Roman Catholic Church. It retained control of much of central Italy. In 1870 troops representing the newly unified nation entered the Vatican and declared it to be subject to the national government. The Popes refused to recognise the authority of the Italian government (or even the existence of the nation), and banned the faithful from holding public office or voting in national elections. In 1929 the Italian ruler Benito Mussolini resolved the dispute by agreeing to pay the Vatican for the loss of its lands, and allowing it to be an independent city-state.

The Church helped form the Christian Democrat party at the end of World War II to represent its interests and to oppose communism. Although the Christian Democrats were Italy's most powerful political party for 50 years, the Church's direct influence began to wane. In 1970, the government made divorce legal, in a decision confirmed by a referendum in 1974. In 1981, a referendum made abortion legal, and in 1984, religious instruction ceased to be compulsory in Italian schools.

In 1990, the State stopped paying the wages of priests, requiring the Church to find the money from donations (Italian tax forms allow taxpayers to stipulate that up to one per cent of their taxes should go to the Catholic Church, but most don't). But the Church cannot cry poor. Its bank has always managed its money effectively, forming some dubious alliances along the way, and in 1998 the consolidated balance sheets of the Holy See showed a profit of $19 million.

Nowadays, 95 per cent of Italians are baptised Catholic, but only 35 per cent practise the religion regularly. It is estimated Italy has 350,000 Protestants, 200,000 Jehovah's Witnesses, and 36,000 Jews.

51
the popes

*t*he Pope is the bishop of Rome, though there's some doubt whether the person usually described as the first Pope, the apostle Peter, was ever there. The first Roman bishop of Rome was a man called Linus, who apparently became leader of the persecuted Christians in 67 AD, when Nero was emperor. From then on the bishops of Rome worked hard to persuade Christian leaders in other cities that Rome was the centre of the Church and that its bishop was 'papa'—father of them all.

This argument became hard to sustain when the Emperor Constantine moved the centre of the empire to Constantinople (now Istanbul, Turkey) in 330, and Rome shrank to a ruined village. But Pope Gregory I, who ruled from 590 to 604, was able to rebuild the power of the Roman Church by sending out missionaries around Europe, paying off the barbarians not to invade, employing an army to expand Church lands, and encouraging tourism to Rome as a fund-raising measure.

In the tenth century the power struggle between the bishops of Rome and the bishops of Constantinople led to a schism wherein Constantinople

RITUALS

became the centre of a new branch of Christianity (now called the Orthodox Church).

The next key Pope was a radical Tuscan monk named Hildebrand who called himself Gregory VII and ruled from 1073 to 1085. He introduced a new militancy in the Church, asserting Rome's right to appoint Church officials (a process which had been abused by the local nobility in many parts of Italy), and argued with various European warlords over separation of Church and state. He excommunicated the Emperor Henry IV, who retaliated by trying to appoint his own Pope and invade Rome.

Pope Urban II showed his influence over European leaders in 1096 by persuading them to carry out the first Crusade into the Holy Land, and later Popes encouraged six more crusades. Pope Innocent III (1198 to 1216) was the most powerful of the medieval Popes, manipulating political events throughout Europe.

For most of the 14th century the Popes lived in Avignon, France, under the control of the French monarchy, and between 1378 and 1417 (the Great Schism) there were three claimants to the Papal throne. The Pope who emerged from the confusion, Martin V, brought the Church's headquarters back to Rome.

An unlikely conversation

Like your new brothel creepers your Holiness?

Good heavens yes, padre. I swear by them

THE 100 THINGS...

In the Renaissance, the Popes, often members of the rich merchant families who controlled the various city-states, functioned as princes, expanding the territory controlled by the Vatican, encouraging the work of artists, and cannibalising the monuments of ancient Rome to build ever more extravagant churches. They also enjoyed wild social lives.

Their extravagance was one of the causes of the Reformation, wherein Christian churches in other European countries rejected papal authority. The Popes responded with a crackdown on dissent within Italy called the Counter-Reformation. In the 19th century, Pope Pius IX opposed all movements towards a united Italy and went into a sulk in 1870 when the Italian government took control of the Papal lands. He and his successors declared themselves to be prisoners within the Vatican until Pius XI reached an agreement with Mussolini that made the Popes rulers of an independent state called Vatican City.

Pope John XXIII was the most loved of this century's popes, forming Vatican Council II in 1960 to modernise Catholic rituals and bring the Church closer to the people. His successor, Paul VI, stopped the reform process and alienated liberal Catholics by issuing an encyclical in 1968 banning all forms of birth control. The Pope who was supposed to reconcile their two approaches, John Paul I, died in 1978 after only a month in office—an event some conspiracy theorists find suspicious in the light of later financial scandals and deaths associated with the Vatican bank.

John Paul II was the first non-Italian to be elected Pope in 500 years. The Italians never let him forget his Polish background, referring to him in the media as *Papa Wojtyla* (pronounced 'woy-teewa'). He has renewed the conservative forces in the Church, diminished the role of the Jesuits (who traditionally were reforming intellectuals), and promoted the fundamentalist Opus Dei movement. He has presided over a period of declining support for Catholicism within Italy and growing support in some Third World countries.

52
crime

*I*taly's annual murder rate of 4.8 per 100,000 looks high by comparison with Australia's (1.8 per 100,000), but remember two factors: the murder rate has dropped from 6.6 per 100,000 in 1990, and most of the murders are part of ongoing warfare between factions within Italy's various mafias and therefore don't impinge on visitors.

As in most countries, the crime most often reported is robbery, though street robbery is at a much lower rate than in America. Visitors are often warned about thieves (called *scippatori*) on motor scooters who zoom past and grab handbags. In 18 visits to Italy I have never seen this happen, but I have often seen another form of robbery, particularly at busy railway stations, wherein groups of gypsies surround travellers and push pieces of paper or cardboard against them, grabbing purses and wallets in the confusion.

Despite the fact that police no longer arrest people for possession of illegal drugs in quantities small enough to be for personal use, drugs are as big a problem for Italy as for any Western country (drug addicts—*tossicodipendenti*—are blamed for most petty theft).

MONEY

53 mafias

*t*here are four main mafias in Italy. The smallest is the **New Holy United Crown of Puglia** in the south-east, which engages in smuggling activities around Bari and has let off several bombs in public places in an effort to frighten off the authorities. Next in size is the *'ndrangheta*, which operates mainly in Calabria and specialises in kidnapping and drug dealing as a source of income (and has links with drug growers in Australia). Its name is supposed to replicate the sound of strumming a guitar.

The *Camorra* of Naples specialises in loan sharking, protection rackets on local shopkeepers and drug dealing, offering employment to thousands of young boys in the Naples back streets. During the 1990s, as a result of the jailing of some Camorra leaders, lower-ranking members of the crime families began shooting each other in an effort to protect their territory and to gain control. In the first six months of 1997, 80 people were killed in street battles. Life became so dangerous in certain suburbs that the

THE 100 THINGS . . .

Italian government sent in the army—300 troops with submachine guns took up positions on key street corners. This sent the murderers indoors.

The biggest organisation is the *Cosa Nostra* of Sicily, which grew out of the self-protection societies which had been operating in Sicily since the Middle Ages. Mussolini cracked down on the Sicilian Mafia, but during World War II its members assisted US troops in their invasion of Sicily, and they became key figures in the rebuilding of Italy after the war.

Because the Mafia was helpful in organising votes for the Christian Democrat Party, its protection rackets, drug dealing and control of the construction industry were left unchecked by the authorities until the mid 1980s, when two investigators, Giovanni Falcone and Paolo Borsellino, prepared a 'maxitrial' which resulted in the jailing of 350 Mafiosi. The investigators were able to use testimony from hundreds of *penitenti*, Mafia members who sought protection from the ruthless faction based in the town of Corleone. They estimated the Mafia's financial turnover at $20 billion a year—the equivalent of Italy's biggest private company, Fiat.

Falcone and Borsellino were both murdered in bomb attacks in the early 1990s, but the head of the Corleone faction, Salvatore Riina, who had gained control of the whole organisation, went on trial for murder in 1993 and is now serving several life sentences. The Mafia has been weakened, but not eliminated.

MONEY

54
the police

*f*or no good reason apart from history, there are four police forces in Italy, with overlapping areas of authority and no interest in mutual cooperation. In descending order of size and efficiency they are:

1. *Carabinieri*. They work for the Ministry of Defence, and are structured like the army. They deal with major crimes against the state, such as the activities of the various mafias. Their uniform is dark blue with a red stripe down the side, with a peaked cap and white leather belt. Their cavalry branch, dressed in capes, swords and knee-high boots, guards national monuments.
2. *La Polizia*. They work for the Ministry of the Interior, and are supposed to investigate large and small crimes and protect VIPs. They wear powder blue pants (sometimes jodhpurs) and navy blazer, unless they are in combat fatigues guarding politically sensitive buildings.
3. *La Guardia di Finanza*. They work for the Ministry of Finance and are interested in tax evasion and smuggling. They wear light grey

THE 100 THINGS ...

uniforms with green berets decorated with a yellow flame symbol.
4. *I Vigili Urbani*. They work for local communes, directing traffic, checking that identity documents are in order, dealing with domestic disputes and minor offences. They wear navy pants and white jackets, with a pith helmet that looks like an English bobby's cap, only white.

If you require assistance from one of these forces (and the *carabinieri* are likely to be the most helpful), you should phone 113.

In addition to these public forces, there are two secret police services operating in Italy: SISDE (*Servizio Informazioni per la Sicurezza Democratica*) and SISMI (*Servizio Informazioni per la Sicurezza Militare*). The first reports to the Minister for the Interior about threats to security within the country, and the second spies on other countries for the Defence Ministry. Both services provide a rich source of material for *dietrologia* (conspiracy theorising) because senior members have been involved in coup plots and violent incidents which they have tried to blame on terrorists.

MONEY

55
the legal system

*t*here are 50,000 people in jail in Italy, but only 23,000 of them have been convicted of anything. The rest are awaiting trial. Italy has more laws per citizen than any other country. Some date back to Roman times, some to the Napoleonic period, and about a third are still on the books from the time of Mussolini (including a law called *vilipendio*, which provides jail terms for 'showing disrespect to national institutions'). It's not surprising then that court proceedings are slow.

It takes an average of seven years to resolve a civil dispute. If you're arrested on a criminal charge, it can take five years to be tried, and another five years to go through the various appeals processes. Here's a typical example: in 1989, a Florence court convicted a group of Mafia members of a train bombing which had taken place in 1984. Then in 1991, their sentences were overturned by the Court of Cassation (an appeals court), which declared there was insufficient evidence. Then in 1993, they were convicted and sentenced again by the Supreme Court.

In major cases, the gathering of evidence is done by *magistrati*—law graduates who must pass tough state exams and then work for a kind of district attorney's office called the *procuratore* in their city. They determine whether a case should be brought to trial, and have the power to detain someone for up to three months without laying a charge, while they conduct interrogations. Once the case goes to court, the magistrate changes from investigator to public prosecutor, arguing the case before a judge.

The magistrates have been the heroes of Italians for the past decade because they have exposed political corruption and mafia activities, often at the cost of their own lives.

ICONS

56
children

*I*taly has a lower proportion of its population under the age of 15 than any country on earth. But that's okay, say the Italians: the fewer kids there are, the more we can spoil them. Some Italians worry that the spoiling process may produce adults who see no reason to deny themselves anything. Gino Martoli, of the research organisation CENSIS, says Italian children are 'hyperstimulated, hypernourished and hyperprotected' and that Italians grow up in a 'sickly sweet infantile environment, out of which only in rare cases do fully formed personalities emerge'. Boys are spoiled for longer than girls—most Italian mothers feel that childhood ends only when a boy does his compulsory 12 months military service at the age of 18. And mum will still do his ironing when he comes back from the army.

Knowing the Italian love of kids, travellers who arrive in Italy with their offspring are surprised at how few public facilities there are for children. There are very few playgrounds in cities and villages, although it's possible to find ancient merry-go-rounds run by chain-smoking entrepreneurs who charge outrageous rates for short rides.

It's also surprising how many children in Italy are forced to work. The trade union grouping CGIL claims there are 300,000 child workers in Italy, mostly in the south. In Naples, where many children work in family cafes, or in factories that make fake designer clothes and accessories, the average wage of a child is $70 a week. A survey conducted in the mid 1990s for the Employment Ministry found that in southern Italy, 30 per cent of boys aged 10 to 14 were in paid employment, even though the legal minimum working age is 15. The government has promised a crackdown.

INSTITUTIONS

57
education

*S*chool exams in Italy are mostly oral, so that being able to spin a good yarn is just as important as knowledge of the facts. One could theorise that this may explain the fluent intellectualism of Italians, both young and old.

By law, Italian children must go to school between the age of six and 14, but 90 per cent of kids between three and six go to a kindergarten, called an *asilo* or a *scuola materna*, either privately run or provided by the local commune. Primary schools (*scuola elementare*) take kids from six to 11, are mostly government run, and offer as core subjects Italian, maths, history and science. Lessons usually go from 8.30 a.m. to 2 p.m., and if parents want kids to do sport or religion, they must organise it themselves, outside those hours.

Junior high school (*scuola media*) takes kids from 11 to 14, and concentrates on Italian literature, history, geography, maths and a foreign language. At the age of 14, 20 per cent of kids leave school, and the others sit a public exam (*diploma di licenza media*) to gain admission to high school (*scuola superiore*). They can then specialise in classical studies (languages, sciences, philosophy, teacher training); technical (preparation for jobs such as accountancy, surveying, hospitality), professional (electronics, chemistry, computers), or artistic (including architecture).

At 18 or 19, students take an exam called *la maturità*, for admission to a university or polytechnic. Tertiary education is free (and for boys, a way of postponing military service).

There are currently about two million tertiary students in Italy, so lecture halls tend to be crowded. It usually takes four years to get a degree. And even at this level, most exams are oral.

RITUALS

58
health

*a*ll Italian citizens are entitled to free basic health care from local GPs, dentists, and hospitals (financed by a health tax). But for serious problems, most prefer to take out insurance to cover private care—partly because it's a status symbol, but mainly because the health system is so chaotic. If they have to go into hospital, they try to have a family member with them at all times, to ensure meals are provided and help can be summoned in an emergency. Medical authorities believe the presence of a family member also promotes healing.

Italians distrust the national health system because they know that university medical schools are overcrowded, doctors can graduate with minimal experience, and hospitals are chronically understaffed. And in the 1990s, as part of the 'Clean Hands' investigations, they learned that the bureaucrat responsible for certifying new medicines as suitable for general release had been taking bribes from drug companies.

But their suspicions don't stop them seeking treatment. In an average month, 25 million Italians see at least one doctor (20 per cent getting a home visit, 70 per cent visiting their GP, and 30 per cent

THE 100 THINGS ...

visiting a specialist). That's one of the world's highest rates of medical servicing.

Disease and supposed miracle cures are the subject of obsessive analysis in everyday conversations. In a survey by the research agency CENSIS, 56 per cent of Italian doctors said they sometimes allowed their patients to tell them what medicine to prescribe. The patients are undeterred by the doctors' habit of administering drugs via the anus. They are surprised that Anglo Saxons prefer to use the mouth.

Italians are fanatical about cleanliness. They spend more on products to scrub themselves, their clothes and their homes than any other nation on earth. The word 'hygeine' can sell anything. Thus toilet paper is called *carta igienica*, and toilet bowls are *servizi igienici*.

And contrary to their stereotype, they are giving up cigarettes, at least in the north. Recent surveys suggest that 28 per cent of Italians are regular smokers—about the same as Australians.

RITUALS

59
death

*t*he main causes of death in Italy, in common with other Western countries, are heart disease and cancer. But Italy's rate of heart disease (55 deaths a year per 100,000) is lower than Australia's (97) and America's (100), which presumably indicates something about the Mediterranean diet. Its rate of suicide is also low (8 per 100,000, compared with 12 in Australia and 10 in the US). The life expectancy for an Italian man nowadays is 75 and for a woman is 82—a little less than the expectancy for Australians.

The commemoration of death is an important ritual for Italians. Most families will hold a wake (*veglia*), during which the body of the deceased is displayed in the house. Funerals are elaborate affairs with expensive floral tributes (usually chrysanthemums) arriving from distant friends and relatives, and black-edged funeral notices pasted up in the streets near the deceased's house. Cremation is rare.

On 1 and 2 November (All Saints Day and The Day of the Dead), vast number of Italians head for cemeteries carrying bunches of chrysanthemums.

RITUALS

60
immigration

*t*he Italian government estimates that there are about a million *extra communitari* (non-Europeans) living in Italy, of whom about 250,000 are illegal. The illegals are mostly young Moroccans working in the fields of the south or the factories of the north-east, doing jobs Italians are no longer keen to do. They need only stay in Italy two years to earn right of residence.

Possibly because of its own history of mass emigration (mainly to America, Australia and South America), Italy has been more tolerant about new arrivals than have most other European nations. There are occasional outbursts by groups calling themselves 'naziskins', and Italians cheerfully make racist jokes about the Africans nicknamed *vu' comprà* ('would you buy') who sell handbags and umbrellas on the footpath, but violence is rare.

The most disliked group are the Gypsies, of whom there are about 100,000 in five tribes (many recently arrived from Yugoslavia). They are stereotyped as surviving primarily by theft, and the stereotype has some basis in fact.

In 1996 a black woman—Denny Mendez, a Caribbean immigrant whose mother had married an Italian—was chosen as Miss Italy on the basis of a majority of votes phoned in to a TV show. This caused much analysis on the talk shows, with the consensus being that although Mendez did not fit 'the Italian standard of beauty', she was chosen because Italians wanted to make a declaration that they are not racist.

STIMULATION

61
the papers

*t*here is no national newspaper for Italy, just 130 dailies originally set up to serve their local areas. But some of the city-based dailies have national impact, particularly Milan's venerable *Corriere della Sera* and Turin's *La Stampa* (both owned by the Fiat company), which have a conservative bias, and Rome's *La Repubblica* and *Il Messagero*, which are more liberal. There is little attempt to distinguish between opinion and factual reporting, and much of the journalism is, by English standards, florid and meandering.

Italians are more united on the daily sports papers, such as *La Gazzetta dello Sport* and *Corriere dello Sport*. *La Gazzetta* sells 700,000 copies a day and a million on Mondays—well ahead of *La Repubblica* or *Corriere della Sera*.

Probably the most respected journalist (in print and on television) in Italy is Milan-based Enzo Biagi, whose book, *Il Boss è Solo* (The Boss is Alone) summarised the mafia 'maxitrials' of the 1980s, and whose *L'Italia dei Peccatori* (The Italy of Sinners) tried in the early 1990s to make sense of the continuing pattern of corruption scandals.

Italy produces an astonishing number of weekly and monthly magazines, mostly published by three companies—Mondadori (owned by Silvio Berlusconi), Rizzoli and Rusconi. The most successful is Berlusconi's weekly gossip and listing magazine *TV Sorrisi e Canzoni* (TV Laughs and Songs), selling 2.4 million copies a week (and always making sure to report the astrological signs of people it discusses). Reflecting the relative preoccupations of Italian men and women, *Quattro Ruote* (Four Wheels) and *Grand Hotel* (a fashion glossy) each sell more than half a million copies a week.

There's a proliferation of literary, artistic and news magazines, of which *Panorama* and *L'Espresso* are the most interesting (*L'Espresso* produces a useful guide to Italy's best restaurants). And there are many gossip weeklies, of which *Gente* and *Oggi* are the least embarrassing, while *Eva Tremila* and *Stop* specialise in distant paparazzi shots of stars seeking privacy, and semi-nude closeups of starlets seeking publicity.

STIMULATION

62
television

*I*talian television started in 1954, and for more than 20 years it was monopolised by the government-owned broadcaster RAI (Radiotelevisione Italia). The traditional division of spoils between the main political parties meant that RAI Uno (specialising in family variety shows) was run by people sympathetic to the Christian Democrats; RAI Due (game shows and documentaries) was biased towards the Socialists and RAI Tre (specialising in talk shows and educational programs) was biased towards the communists. The political directions of the RAI stations have broken down during the 1990s, along with the parties they used to promote.

In the 1980s the real estate mogul Silvio Berlusconi bought a lot of local commercial stations and welded them into three national networks: Canale 5 (specialising in soap operas), Rete 4 (movies and game shows such as 'La ruota della fortuna'—The Wheel of Fortune—and 'Okay! il prezzo e giusto'—The Price is Right), and Italia 1 (more youth-oriented, with rock videos, 'I Simpson', and 'Melrose Place'). American soap operas are hugely popular, especially 'Beautiful', the Italian name for the daytime series 'The Bold and the Beautiful'.

STIMULATION

What strikes the visitor most on Italian television is the high bimbo count. Gorgeous women with long shiny hair are everywhere—on game shows, science documentaries, variety shows, talk shows and the news. The most astonishing program is 'Colpo Grosso' (Big Hit) which involves quiz contestants taking off their clothes or nominating a stripper to take off her clothes for each correct answer.

The most popular variety programs (usually on Sunday night) include 'Creme Caramel' (starring former Miss Italy Pamela Prati as singer and presenter) and 'Fantastico!' (featuring a local rapper called Giovanotte). The big names on the chat shows are Maurizio Constanzo and Mara Venier.

The most legendary figure on Italian television is Mike Bongiorno, who has been hosting game and variety shows since the 1950s, first on RAI and then (purchased at great expense) on Berlusconi's networks. He is famous for having said, when a female contestant made a mistake on a question about a bird, *'la signora mi e caduta sull' uccello'*, which he intended to mean 'the lady has fallen down on the bird' but which can also mean 'the lady has gone down on my dick'.

63
cinema

*I*taly was a world pioneer in the film business, and in the English-speaking world, it is famous for being 'arty'. In fact, most of Italy's breakthroughs were on what serious film scholars would consider the frivolous fringe of the industry.

Italy's first film studio, Cines Caesar, was set up in 1905, and made the world's first international blockbuster, *Quo Vadis*, which was the *Titanic* of its day. In 1906 the world's first movie theme music was composed by Romolo Bacchini for the movie *Malia dell'Oro*, and Italy became the first country where major films were regularly accompanied by an original score (America didn't start this detail till the 1920s).

The first awards for feature length films were given at the International Exhibition in Turin in 1912, just six years after the world's first feature film was shown (*The Story of the Kelly Gang*, in Australia) and 17 years before the first Academy Awards.

A million dollar desert-and-mountain spectacular called *Cabiria*, two years in the making, became a big hit in the US in 1914 and was a major influence on the later works of D. W. Griffith and Cecil B.

DeMille. The world's first regular film festival started at the Hotel Excelsior in Venice in August, 1932 (and continues in Venice to this day).

In the 1930s, Mussolini set up the Cinecittà studios just outside Rome, and after the war they became a little Hollywood (used even for such American productions as *Ben Hur* and *Cleopatra*). Italy found worldwide success with sexy movies that could be marketed as 'arthouse' because they were in a foreign language (at a time when American films were inhibited by 'family values'). The prototype was *Bitter Rice* in 1949, which introduced voluptuous Silvana Mangano. She was followed by Gina Lollobrigida (*Bread, Love and Dreams* in 1953) and Sophia Loren (*Aida* in 1953). Their male equivalent was Marcello Mastroianni, who first charmed international audiences in 1952 with *Sensualita*.

Once cinemagoers got beyond the nudity, they discovered the ingenuity of Italian directors, and the techniques of 'neorealist' film-makers such as Michelangelo Antonioni, Federico Fellini, Vittorio de Sica, and Luchino Visconti became hugely influential around the world. In the 1960s, some Italian directors threw aside the arty reputation and had fun with what came to be called 'sword and sandal epics' (such as the *Hercules* series, starring Steve Reeves) and 'spaghetti westerns' (such as *The Good, The Bad and The Ugly*, starring Clint Eastwood and directed by Sergio Leone, who went on to make the gangster epic *Once Upon A Time In America*).

After Sophia Loren and Marcello Mastroanni, Italians have made heroes of four comic actors: Totò, a music hall clown from Naples who became Italy's Charlie Chaplin with a stream of slapstick hits in the 1950s; Alberto Sordi, a Roman with a specialty in wry taxi driver characters; Ugo Tognazzi, a suave stylist from Cremona best known for *La Cage Aux Folles* and Bertolucci's *Tragedy of a Ridiculous Man*; and Roberto Benigni, a rubber faced improviser who got noticed in America in the deadpan films of Jim Jarmusch and who directed and starred in *Life is Beautiful* in 1997. The mogul who matters in the 1990s is Vittorio Cecchi Gori, who finances most of the Italian-made movies and distributes most of the foreign-made ones.

Nowadays Italians buy 92 million movie tickets a year (compared with 28 million tickets for live performances) but their allegiance is shifting away from their own creations to the Hollywood mass market spectaculars. Cinecitta studios are often empty. Italy's highest grossing movie of all time is *Titanic*.

PASSIONS

64
the top films

*h*ere's a short list of movies that offer an insight into the Italian psyche or into the art of film-making ...

Ossessione (1942). The first film by Luchino Visconti, it's a raw adaptation of the US novel *The Postman Always Rings Twice*, and is said to have started the 'neorealist' wave.

Open City (*Roma, Citta Aperto*, 1945). Directed by Roberto Rossellini and starring Anna Magnani, it's the story of Italian resistance fighters during the German occupation of Rome.

Shoeshine (*Sciuscia*, 1946). Directed by Vittorio De Sica, it's a tough look at delinquent teens in war-ravaged Rome, and won a special Oscar before there was any 'Best Foreign Film' category.

Paisan (*Paisa*, 1946). Directed by Rossellini and co-written by Federico Fellini, it tells six short stories of the Allied advance through Italy.

The Bicycle Thief (*Ladri di Biciclette*, 1948). Directed by De Sica, it's about a bill-poster and his son desperately searching Rome's back streets for a stolen bike, and it won a special Oscar.

La Strada (1954). Directed by Fellini and starring his wife Giulietta Masina and Anthony Quinn, it's about a circus strongman who mistreats his simpleminded wife, and won Best Foreign Film Oscar.

La Dolce Vita (1960). Directed by Fellini and starring Marcello Mastroianni and Anita Ekberg, it's about a gossip columnist who follows an American star through Rome's nightlife. The name of the photographer—Paparazzo—became generic.

L'Avventura (1961). Directed by Michelangelo Antonioni, it's about socialites searching for (but not finding) a girl who goes missing during a swimming party.

Two Women (*La Ciociara*, 1961). Directed by De Sica and starring Sophia Loren (who won a Best Actress Oscar), it's about a mother and daughter who are raped as they try to escape the war.

8½ (*Otto e Mezzo*, 1963). Directed by Fellini and starring Mastroianni and Claudia Cardinale, it's about a director's problems in completing a film, and won the best Foreign Film Oscar.

The Leopard (*Il Gattopardo*, 1963). Directed by Visconti and starring Burt Lancaster, it's about Sicilian aristocrats adjusting to the unification of Italy in 1860, with an hour-long banquet scene.

Yesterday, Today and Tomorrow (*Ieri, Oggi, Domani*, 1963). Directed by De Sica, it contains three short comedies in which Loren and Mastroianni explore romantic permutations, and won a Foreign Film Oscar.

Romeo and Juliet (*Romeo e Giuletta*, 1968).

Directed by Franco Zeffirelli, who used unknown teenagers to make the lovers more innocent.

The Damned (*La Caduta Degli Dei*, 1969). Directed by Visconti and starring Dirk Bogarde, it's about how a family running steel factories helped the rise of Hitler.

The Conformist (*Il Conformista*, 1970). Directed by Bernardo Bertolucci, it's a portrait of an assassin working for the Fascist party.

Death in Venice (*Morte a Venezia*, 1971). Directed by Visconti and starring Bogarde, it's a portrait of an ageing composer who fancies a 14 year old boy.

Amarcord (1974). It's Fellini's recollection of hilarious and tragic episodes from his childhood in a seaside village.

Bread and Chocolate (*Pane e Cioccolata*, 1974). Directed by Franco Brusati, it's the adventures of a southern Italian who seeks work as a waiter in a Swiss resort.

Seven Beauties (*Pasqualino Settebellezze*, 1974). Directed by Lina Wertmuller, it's about two Italian deserters trying to survive in a German concentration camp.

1900 (*Novocento*, 1976). Directed by Bertolucci and starring Robert De Niro, it's a 300 minute epic about social turmoil in Italy.

Allegro non troppo (1977). Directed by Bruno Bozzetto, it's a brilliantly animated parody of *Fantasia*.

THE 100 THINGS ...

Padre Padrone (1977). Directed by the twins Paolo and Vittorio Taviani, it's about a boy's triumph over his Sardinian peasant background.

To Forget Venice (*Dementicare Venezia*, 1979). Directed by Brusati, it's about complex family and other relationships on a country estate near Venice.

The Tree of Wooden Clogs (*L'Albero degli Zoccoli*, 1978). Directed by Ermanno Olmi, it's about peasant families in Lombardy in 1896.

Night of the Shooting Stars (*La Notte di San Lorenzo*, 1983). Directed by the Taviani brothers, it's about resisting the Fascists and the Germans in a Tuscan village in 1944.

Ginger and Fred (1986). Directed by Fellini and starring his wife Masina and Mastroianni, it's a satire on television and how it corrupts the reunion of a dancing duo.

Cinema Paradiso (1988). Directed by Giuseppe Tornatore, it's a celebration of the joy of movies through the story of a small boy and a blinded projectionist in a Sicilian village.

Mediterraneo (1991). Directed by Gabriele Salvatores, it's about Italian soldiers supposedly controlling a Greek island during the war.

STIMULATION

65 writers

*t*hese, in roughly chronological order, are the names an educated Italian knows as literary giants ...

Julius Caesar, whose commentaries on the Gallic Wars and the Roman Civil Wars offer insights not only into the history of the first century BC but also the military mind.

Virgil, who wrote the epic poem *The Aeneid* around 30 BC, and connected the destruction of Troy with the founding of Rome.

Ovid, whose *Amores* poems dealt with lust and seduction and whose *Metamorphoses* provided stories reused by authors for the following 2000 years.

Petronius, who satirised the excesses of Nero's Rome in *Satyricon*.

Tacitus, whose *Histories and Annals* (written around 100 AD) provide juicy gossip on the emperors.

Dante Alighieri, whose *Divine Comedy* (see next chapter) is the most studied book in the world after the Bible, and whose *De Vulgari Eloquentia* discussed the diversity of Italian dialects in the 14th century.

THE 100 THINGS . . .

Francesco Petrarca, who is best known for 350 sonnets in honour of Laura, a married woman he had loved in his youth, and whose work inspired Shakespeare.

Giovanni Boccacio, who is best known for *The Decameron*, 100 folk tales supposedly told by young men and women escaping the plague of Florence in 1348, which influenced Chaucer.

Niccolò Machiavelli, who satirised religious corruption in his play *La Mandragola*, and is considered the founder of modern political theory for his books *Arte della Guerra* (Art of War) and *Il Principe* (The Prince).

Torquato Tasso, who produced, in the late 16th century, the heroic poem *Gerusalemme Liberata* (Jerusalem Liberated) about the conquest of Christ's sepulchre during the Crusades.

Carlo Goldoni, who created the comedy of character in the late 18th century with stage plays such as *Il Ventaglio* about Venice society.

Alessandro Manzoni, who pioneered the Italian novel in 1827 with *I Promessi Sposi* (The Betrothed).

Giacomo Leopardi, an anguished romantic of the mid 19th century who is regarded as Italy's greatest lyric poet after Dante.

Giosuè Carducci, who won the Nobel Prize in 1906 for poems about his disillusionment with the politics of newly united Italy.

Gabriele d'Annunzio, whose poems about sex and sensuousness and whose 1889 novel *Il Piacere*

(Pleasure) made him leader of the Decadent movement.

Carlo Collodi (real name Lorenzini), whose story of Pinocchio, published in 1911, gave the world a new fairytale.

Tommaso Marinetti, whose poetry of the 1920s gloried in speed, machinery and the cult of Futurism.

Luigi Pirandello, whose plays, such as *Six Characters in Search of an Author*, explored loneliness and difficulties of communication.

Antonio Gramsci, who went to jail for writing left-wing political arguments during the Fascist period.

Alberto Moravia, a 'neo-realist' who revived the Italian novel with *Gli Indifferenti* (Time of Indifference), which was censored for attacking fascism.

Italo Calvino, the pioneer of 'postmodern magic realism' after World War II, with playful novels such as *If on a Winter's Night a Traveller*, about the urge to read.

Giuseppe Tomasi di Lampedusa, who wrote *Il Gattopardo* (The Leopard) about Sicilian corruption.

Umberto Eco, whose novel *The Name of the Rose*, a political satire disguised as a murder mystery, was an international hit.

THE 100 THINGS ...

Dario Fò, a satirical playwright best known for *Accidental Death of an Anarchist*, who won the 1997 Nobel Prize for literature (worth $1.4 million) because 'his strength is the creation of texts that simultaneously amuse, engage and provide perspectives'. Fò says of Italians: 'We are a civilised and generous people. All you have to do is look at how we maintain our public servants.'

STIMULATION

66
the book

*i*f you added together the attention paid to *Hamlet*, *Macbeth*, *Pride and Prejudice* and *Oliver Twist* in the schools of the English-speaking world, you would still not come near measuring the role of the epic poem *La Divina Commedia* in Italian schools. Since they study it for several years, most adult Italians can quote chunks of it verbatim.

The Divine Comedy is a commentary on its time (around 1300); a demand for social reform; a summary of how philosophy, science, history and theology were understood then; and the first great work of Italian literature written in the language actually spoken by the people of Florence, rather than in Latin. It came to define what is now the standard form of the Italian language. And it is the world's longest love letter, from Dante to Beatrice, a girl he'd admired from afar since they were both nine (and who was dead by the time he wrote the poem).

The Divine Comedy is the story of a sinner's journey through Hell (*Inferno*) and Purgatory (*Purgatorio*) until he reaches Heaven (*Paradiso*). First the ancient Roman poet Virgil guides the sinner down through the ten circular layers of Hell.

At the bottom is Satan, up to his waist in ice and gnawing at the greatest traitors in history: Judas, Brutus and Cassius, the assassins of Julius Caesar. (Dante's consignment of some of the prominent figures of his day to various layers of Hell has influenced many modern comedians, most recently Woody Allen in *Deconstructing Harry*).

Then the sinner climbs the seven hills of Mount Purgatory (each representing a cardinal sin), and meets a new guide, Beatrice, who takes him on a space odyssey via the moon, planets and stars to a final vision of God.

STIMULATION

67
art

*U*NESCO estimates that two thirds of the world's art treasures are in Italy, with three internationally admired paintings, sculptures or buildings for every citizen. So do you seriously expect me to summarise Italy's art in one chapter? Of course you do, since that's what this book is all about ...

Italy's oldest surviving art is a bunch of carvings on the rock walls of the Camonica valley, north of Lake Iseo in Lombardy. They are between 4000 and 3000 years old and show scenes of hunting and fighting. The whole area has been turned into a national park (Parco Nationale delle Incisionie Ruprestri di Naquane).

The Etruscans of the 7th century BC were art lovers, and their legacy is the graceful paintings of everyday life on the walls of burial chambers at Cerveteri and Tarquinia (both in Lazio, north of Rome). The Romans initially copied the art style of the Etruscans and the Greeks, doing frescoes of pleasant landscapes in wet plaster on the walls of their villas. Their sculptures were mostly for propaganda—to celebrate military victories or to make their emperors look like mythical heroes.

THE 100 THINGS . . .

Then towards the end of the empire, the Romans got fascinated by mosaics—pictures made from little bits of coloured stone. The fad reached its peak in the 5th century at Ravenna (the Mausoleum of Galla Placidia is the supreme example) with influences from Byzantium and a content dictated by the Christian Church—the life and death of Jesus or the martyrdom of various saints. But these themes got pretty repetitive over the next 500 years, since the people represented in church frescoes all looked alike and the backgrounds were minimal (because the Church considered it immoral to try to represent reality).

The breakthrough came at the end of the 13th century, when two Florentine artists, Giovanni Cimabué and his pupil Giotto di Bondone, started trying to represent religious stories in a naturalistic way (to look like real people in real landscapes). Both of them did frescoes in the church of St Francis in Assisi, and Giotto's frescoes in the Bargello in Florence cheekily included images of local identities such as Dante.

As artists gained the support of rich merchant families in the 14th century, they were able to stray from the limits imposed by the Church. They began to do portraits of their patrons instead of the saints, and to wrestle with the problems of perspective.

The big names around Florence were Michelangelo Buonarrotti, Leonardo da Vinci and Raphael (Raffaelo Santi), while the most influential sculptor was Donatello (Donato di Betto Bardi). In Venice during the 15th century, Jacopo Bellini and his son Giovanni did amazing things with light and colour in landscape paintings, and were then surpassed by Giorgione (Giorgio Barbarelli), who introduced the notion of the easel painting, designed to hang on the wall of a private home as a decoration rather than a religious inspiration.

One of Giorgione's students, Titian (Tiziano Vecellio) introduced a richness of colour to mythological subjects and inspired the next generation of artists such as Caravaggio (Michelangelo Merisi) and Annibale Carraci in a flamboyant style that came to be called Baroque.

Those who like labels use Rococo for the next phase of Italian art, typified by Giam Battista Tiepolo, working in Venice in the early 18th century, while another Venetian, Antonio Canova, pioneered a graceful new style of sculpture in the 1780s with works such as *Theseus* and *Cupid and Psyche*.

They were the last of the geniuses for 150 years. Early in the 20th century, Italian painters and sculptors, inspired by the poet Marinetti, introduced a style called Futurism, which celebrated speed, machines and crowds. The biggest names of recent years have been Amadeo Modigliani (died in 1920), whose long angular faces look like alien sightings, and Giorgio di Chirico (died in 1978), who was one of the pioneering surrealists.

STIMULATION

68
architecture

*t*he Romans were the master engineers of the ancient world, and they're credited with inventing concrete, the dome and the arch. They were also thoughtful town planners, recognising the need for a central square in every town, where people could meet, shop, eat and argue. Around the forums they built public baths which also served as gymnasiums, casinos, libraries, and leisure centres. For mass entertainment they built amphitheatres, with adjustable awnings to protect spectators from sun and rain.

The Roman forums evolved into the piazzas of medieval towns, while their temples, with awesome interior spaces, adapted easily to hold the Christian mass.

Scholars like to divide the architectural phases that followed the **Classical Period** (0 to 400 AD) into the **Byzantine Period** (500 to 800), in which eastern influences are apparent (examples: the San Vitale church in Ravenna and the cupolas on St Mark's in Venice); the **Romanesque Period** (800 to 1200), in which Roman ruins were robbed to make new decorative elements in churches and civic buildings (examples: the cathedral and the leaning tower in

STIMULATION

Pisa's Field of Miracles); the **Renaissance Period** (1200 to 1600), when artists became architects and individual imagination was rewarded by merchant princes (examples: the Duomo in Florence and the Tempietto di San Pietro in Montorio, Rome); the **Baroque Period** (1600 to 1700), in which the Church was reasserting its authority and encouraging architects to decorate more lavishly, often with exaggerated curves (example: much of St Peter's in Rome); the **Rococo Period** (1700 to 1800), which was French-influenced and extravagant (example: Rome's Trevi fountain); and the **Modern Period** (1800 to the present), which covers bits of art nouveau in the 19th century (Milan's Galleria), the sleek style of the 1920s called *razionalismo*, the imposing masses of the Fascist years (Milan's central railway station) and the elegant postwar steel and concrete skyscrapers of Milan and Turin.

The names to know in Italian architecture are:

Hadrian. More of a property developer than an emperor, he started a massive building program when he took the throne in 117 AD, most notably the Temple of Venus and Rome in the Forum, the Pantheon with its huge dome, and his mausoleum,

...And God saw the world that He had made, and realised it could do with a little reworking...

which became the Castel Sant'Angelo, a fortress for the Popes. He toured his empire, gathering ideas in Germany, France, Spain and Britain (where he built a wall from Solway to Tyne) and on his return, he built a villa complex with gardens and fountains at Tivoli, just outside Rome.

Filippo Brunelleschi. First a goldsmith, then a sculptor, he designed the ribbed dome for Florence's Cathedral in 1420 (it still has the largest diameter of any dome in the world) and then the churches of Spirito Santo and San Lorenzo in Florence. His sense of geometric proportions dominated Italian architecture for centuries.

Michelangelo. Pope Julius II commissioned him in 1503 to design a papal tomb, and Michelangelo worked on the project for 40 years, constantly being interrupted by details such as painting the ceiling of the Sistine Chapel (for which Michelangelo had recommended Raphael) and designing St Peter's. The papal tomb was never finished, but the Big M is known for the Laurentian Library in Florence and the Piazza of the Campidoglio in Rome.

Andrea Palladio. Born in Vicenza, northern Italy, he created a new style for non-church buildings in the mid 16th century, using ancient Roman temples as the inspiration for his palaces and villas. He is best known for the Teatro Olimpico and the Villa Rotunda at Vicenza, and Villa Foscari at Malcontenta.

Giovanni Bernini. The first major baroque

sculptor and designer, he is best known for the four rivers fountain in Piazza Navona (1647), the apse of St Peter's and the colonnade in front of it, and the grand staircase to the Vatican.

Francesco Borromini. A stone-cutter and student of Bernini, he developed the baroque style in the early 17th century, worked on the rebuilding of St Peter's, and is best known for the San Carlo alle Quattro Fontane church in Rome.

Giuseppe Terragni. The leader of a 1920s design movement in Como that some called modern and some called fascist, Terragni issued a manifesto that attacked neo-classical and neo-baroque styles. He's best known for the Casa del Fascio (now called Casa del Popolo) in Como.

Marcello Piacentini. He was director of monumental projects intended by Mussolini to inspire awe and patriotism, such as the Rome suburb called EUR and the sports complex called Foro Italico.

Pier Luigi Nervi. Professor of Engineering at Rome University between 1946 and 1961, his experiments with reinforced concrete in the Exhibition Buildings in Turin and the Stadiums for the 1960 Rome Olympics brought him world acclaim. Nervi revived the ancient Roman notion that bold engineering is at the heart of great architecture. He was jointly responsible, with Giò Ponti, for Milan's elegant Pirelli skyscraper, and was engineering consultant on Harry Seidler's Sydney buildings the MLC Centre and Australia Square.

THE 100 THINGS ...

Gae Aulenti. Trained in Milan, and best known for the conversion during the 1980s of a beaux-arts railway station into Paris's Musee d'Orsay, she's as famous in Italy for industrial and interior design as for architecture.

Romaldo Giurgola. Rome-born (1920) and trained partly in the USA, he is best known outside Italy for the new Parliament House in Canberra.

Renzo Piano. Trained in Genoa and Milan, Piano introduced a high-tech look to modern architecture in the 1970s, most notably with the Pompidou Centre in Paris. Now part of a company called Studio Nuovo, he is designing a new State Office Block for Sydney.

STIMULATION

69
music

*t*he ancient Etruscans made music part of everything. Their wall paintings show flautists accompanying the hunt, apparently to entice the animals to their doom. Music has dominated Italian life ever since.

Italians invented the violin (1550), the piano (1709), the musical scale, the madrigal, the opera, the sonata, the concerto, the symphony, and the system of musical notation which has now become the world standard. Opera fills chapter 70, but the names to know in other kinds of Italian music are ...

Francesco Landini, a blind organist in 14th century Florence, whose 'Ecco la Primavera' ('Here is the Spring') is the most famous of his 54 collections of songs.

Giovanni Palestrina, a choirmaster and furrier in 16th century Rome, who wrote 105 masses and many motets and madrigals.

Giovanni Gabrieli, who was called 'the musical Titian of Venice' in the early 17th century, because of the richness of the harmonies in his choral music.

Arcangelo Corelli, working in Rome in the late 17th century, who produced the first successful sonatas for violin and harpsichord and developed the form called *concerto grosso* for chamber orchestras.

Antonio Vivaldi, a Venetian choirmaster of the early 18th century, who wrote more than 400 concertos, and is best known for 'The Four Seasons'.

Domenico Scarlatti, a Neapolitan harpsichordist of the early 18th century, who perfected the sonata form.

Nicolò Paganini, a Genoese violin virtuoso of the early 19th century, who could play so fast and create such audience hysteria he was said to be in league with the devil.

Ennio Morricone, one of the supreme film composers of the late 20th century, he scored the music of films such as *Cinema Paradiso*, *The Mission*, and *1900*.

These days, Naples keeps up its reputation for musical innovation by being the home of Italy's tiny rock scene. You can hear rock music all over Italy— even talk radio stations play it between midnight and dawn and there are six TV networks devoted to rock videos—but most of it is American. Italy's tastes in popular music tend to the sentimental, as displayed in the winning songs each February at the San Remo pop festival, and the mass-market singers are clean and well-groomed. The *romanticoni* are middle-aged, often balding performers who write and sing songs about mothers, lovers and their local neighbourhoods.

STIMULATION

The biggest names of the 1990s are Zucchero (Sugar, which is an appropriate description), the white rapper Jovanotti, Mina (Italy's answer to Barbra Streisand), Gianni Nini, Laura Pausini and the bands called 883 (pronounced Otto Otto Tre, with a big hit called 'Come Mai') and 99 Posse (pronounced Ninedy Nine Possay). The song every Italian pop singer knows is 'Volare'.

STIMULATION

70
opera

*I*taly invented opera in the 16th century, perfected it in the 18th, and turned a tenor into a superstar in the 20th. Opera developed from singing shows put on for the wedding feasts of rich families in Florence in the late 16th century. A group of intellectuals called the Camerata were experimenting with setting ancient Greek dramas to music, and the first complete opera that resulted from this—*Dafne* by Jacopo Peri—was performed at the Palazzo Corsi in Florence early in 1597. It was a flop, but the idea took off when Claudio Monteverdi, the court composer in Mantua, included humour and love scenes in a drama called *Orfeo*, first performed in Mantua in 1607. Venice became the hot opera centre until Monteverdi's death in 1643, when Naples took over until it was itself superceded by Milan in the 19th century. The names to know are . . .

Alessandro Scarlatti, working in Naples in the early 1700s, who established the operatic structure that is now most familiar: an overture played by a string orchestra, followed by sung narrative (recitative) interrupted by regular arias where

STIMULATION

performers get to show off their skills. *La Griselda* was his biggest hit.

Gioachino Rossini, who developed the lighter style called *opera buffa* with *The Barber of Seville* in 1816 and got serious with *William Tell* in 1829.

Vincenzo Bellini, best known for *Norma* (1831) and **Gaetano Donizetti**, best known for *Lucia di Lammermoor* (1835), who were the pioneers of a lively singing style called *bel canto*.

Giuseppe Verdi, who worked in Milan and poured out *Rigoletto*, *Il Trovatore*, *La Traviata*, *Aida*, *Otello* and *Falstaff* between 1851 and 1893. He became associated with the struggle for unification of Italy, with 'Viva Verdi' a code for 'Viva Vittorio Emanuele Re d'Italia' (Long live Victor Emanuel, King of Italy).

Pietro Mascagni, who wrote *Cavalleria Rusticana* in 1890 (about passion in Sicily) and **Ruggero**

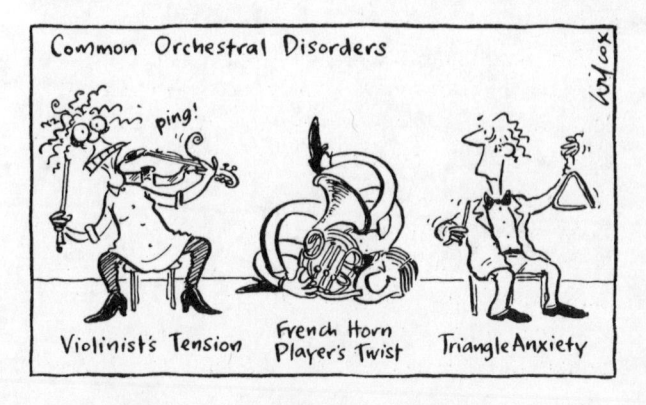

Leoncavallo, who wrote *Pagliacci* in 1892 (about a murderous clown). Being short, 'Cav and Pag' are often performed together.

Giacomo Puccini, who introduced *verismo* (social issues) into works such as *La Boheme*, *Madama Butterfly*, and *The Girl of the Golden West* between 1896 and 1910.

Luciano Berio, a modern composer (born 1925) who has experimented with the forms of opera and music theatre in works such as *Un Re in Ascolto*.

And then, of course, there's **Luciano Pavarotti,** the balsamic tenor from Modena who brought operatic arias to the masses during the 1980s and made himself an international pop star.

The best theatres in which to see opera in Italy nowadays are La Scala in Milan (opened 1778), San Carlo in Naples (opened 1737) and La Fenice in Venice (1792).

PIONEERS

71
science

*P*erhaps we shouldn't count Archimedes as the first Italian scientist, since Syracuse in Sicily was a Greek colony when he was living there in 250 BC (and he was killed by an invading Roman). But with inquiring Renaissance minds like Leonardo da Vinci and Galileo, Italy needs no help in establishing its scientific credentials. More recently, Evangelista Toricelli developed the barometer in Florence in 1644; Domenico Cassini perfected the telescope while Professor of Astronomy at Bologna University in the 1660s; Alessandro Volta invented the electric battery and demonstrated it to Napoleon in 1801; Guglielmo Marconi invented the first practical system for sending radio signals and won a Nobel Prize in 1909; and Enrico Fermi built the world's first practical nuclear reactor at the University of Chicago and won a Nobel Prize in 1938.

These days, Italians complain that neither industry nor government spends enough on scientific research, with the result that Italy has only three per cent of the patents registered in Europe. The next lowest in patents, with five per cent, is Switzerland. This recalls the comparison made by

THE 100 THINGS ...

Orson Welles, speaking as Harry Lime in the movie *The Third Man*: 'In Italy for 30 years under the Borgias they had warfare, terror, murder, bloodshed. They produced Michelangelo, Leonardo da Vinci and the Renaissance. In Switzerland, they had brotherly love, 500 years of democracy and peace. And what did they produce? The cuckoo clock.' Perhaps Italy is too peaceful these days.

Note: Galileo's right-hand middle finger is preserved in a bottle in Florence's science museum.

PIONEERS

72 firsts

*t*he Italians have been prolific inventors—but then, they've had a lot of history within which to be creative. Here are a few of their breakthroughs...

Airmail stamps were issued by the Italian post office in 1917, marked *Esperimento Posta Aerea*, for the service between Turin and Rome.

The scientific study of **anatomy** was initiated in the 1740s by Giovanni Battista Morgagni of Padua, the first pathologist and the author of *The Causes of Illnesses Investigated by Anatomy*.

Artificial insemination was first done by Lazare Spallanzani of Rome in 1779, when he injected the semen of a spaniel into a female hunting dog, who produced three puppies 62 days later.

The **condom** was invented by Gabriel Fallopius, professor of anatomy at Padua University, in 1562. It was a linen sheath worn over the end of the penis to prevent venereal disease (preventing conception was a bonus).

The first **cremation device**, an open furnace incinerator, was designed by Dr L. Brunetti of Padua and used to cremate the body of a 35 year old woman in 1869. Brunetti demonstrated an improved model at the Vienna exhibition of 1873.

Dissection of human bodies was initiated by surgeons at the medical school of Salerno in 1235.

Double entry bookkeeping was first expounded by Lucas Paciolus in Venice in 1495.

The **espresso machine** in the form we know it was invented in 1946 by Achille Gaggia (though the steam nozzle for frothing milk had been in use since 1907).

The **fax machine** was developed by Giovanni Caselli in Florence in 1864, and named the Pantelegraph. It used an electrically charged pendulum which scanned the text and converted it to pulses. By 1868 it was able to transmit 110 fax pages an hour over the telegraph line between Paris and Lyons, and could send engravings and technical drawings with great accuracy.

Glass eyes were created by Ambroise Pare in Venice in 1578.

The **glass paperweight** was introduced by Pierre Rigaglia in Venice in 1845.

The first **income tax** in the world seems to have been the *catastro* introduced in Florence under Lorenzo di Medici in 1451.

The first flashing **indicator lights** were introduced in Fiat cars in 1935.

The **insurance policy** (from the word *polizza*, a promise or undertaking) was introduced to England by merchants representing the Pope in the 14th century.

The **internal combustion engine** (gas-powered)

PIONEERS

was designed by Eugenio Barsanti and Felice Matteuci in Florence in 1853, and installed at the Maria Antonia Railway Station in 1856.

The first **inter-city motorway** was the autostrada between Milan and Varese, opened by the King of Italy in 1924 (soon becoming part of a 54-mile network with 33 viaducts and 56 tunnels).

The first mass production **pasta factory** was started by Paolo Agnesi in Imperia in 1824.

Planes were first used in warfare by two Italian pilots who flew over a Turkish encampment in a Bleriot XI on 23 October 1911, doing aerial reconnaissance during the Italo-Turkish war.

Painted **theatre scenery** (a backdrop of houses) was first used in a play called *Cassaria* at Ferrara in 1508.

The **seismograph**, for recording earthquakes, was invented by Luigi Palmieri in 1855.

Spectacles were apparently invented in Italy in the 1280s, and were first described by an author named Sandro di Popozo, who wrote in 1289: 'Without the glasses known as spectacles, I would no longer be able to read and write'.

The first **telephone** that could transmit speech by electronic impulses was tested in 1849 by Antonio Meucci of Florence between the basement and the third floor of his house in Havana, Cuba.

The first purpose-built **indoor theatre** was the Teatro Olimpico in Vicenza, designed by Palladio in 1580.

THE 100 THINGS ...

The first **typewriter** was built in 1808 by Pellegrine Turri of Reggio Emilia for a blind friend, containing 23 letters of the Italian alphabet and four punctuation marks.

The first **watch** was mentioned in a letter dated November 1462, when the clockmaker Bartholomew Manfredi wrote to the Marchese di Manta offering to make him a 'pocket clock' better than the Duke of Modena's.

The first **weather bureau** was set up in Tuscany by Luigi Antinori in 1654, taking daily temperature readings and collating information from observers in Parma, Milan, Bologna and Florence.

The first **woman university graduate** was Elena Cornaro of Venice, who was granted a doctorate of philosophy by the University of Padua in 1678. She had not been allowed to attend lectures, but had been privately tutored. The first woman to study at a university on the same basis as men was Laura Bassi, who graduated in philosophy at the University of Bologna in 1732. She became the first woman to teach in a university, joining the faculty and lecturing in philosophy from 1732 to 1778.

RITUALS

73
comedy

*i*n the 16th century Italians got interested in a kind of travelling pantomime called *la commedia dell'arte*, a form which influenced the way comic theatre developed throughout Europe and gave birth to vaudeville in Britain and America. It explains what makes Italians laugh nowadays. A group of travelling players would arrive in a town, quickly familiarise themselves with the current gossip and politics, and then incorporate what they'd learned into a slapstick show. The broad plot and the masked characters stayed the same, but within that structure, the actors would improvise to suit each new audience.

The crucial element was Italian regional stereotyping—the conviction that someone's personality is shaped by where he or she comes from—which let the actors quickly establish the characters with each new audience. Thus the character called The Doctor (often Dottore Balanzone) spoke in the dialect of Bologna, which told audiences he was scholarly, lustful, talkative and a glutton. His mask had a bulbous nose.

The servant called Brighella came from Bergamo, where people are crafty and coarse, and his aim is 'to outwit an old lovesick fool, to rob a miser'.

Another side of Bergamo was shown in Arlecchino, who is also clever, but is more cheerful, and who feigns simplicity to get out of scrapes. Brighella's target for con tricks was often Pantalone, a merchant from Venice, greedy, pompous, quarrelsome, and, like his home city, once wealthy, now fallen on hard times.

Pulcinella came from Naples, often with a hunchback and a long nose, and was an opportunist—dishonest but kind-hearted. Meneghino was a money-lover from Milan, Rugantino was a lazy pragmatist from Rome. And The Captain (often called Scaramuccia) was a bragging soldier from Spain, the country which had occupied Italy shortly before the *commedia* became fashionable.

By the end of the 18th century, *la commedia dell'arte* had ceased to exist as a touring display of improvisation, because audiences preferred formally scripted plays such as those by Goldoni. But its traditions flowed into the music halls, flourishing in Rome and Naples early this century, and are obvious nowadays in sketches and standup routines performed on Italian television. The comedian's dialect and his body language establishes immediately his place of origin. Thus Roberto Benigni is seen as a Tuscan, Massimo Troisi as a Neapolitan and Renato Pozzetto as a Milanese. They may no longer wear masks, but their audiences know just what to expect, and they laugh when their expectations are confirmed or twisted.

RITUALS

74
campanilismo

*I*talians are highly patriotic, but not to their country. It is the neighbourhood that matters most (after the family, of course). You know that your part of town is superior to all others, and that your city is superior to all others, and that your region is superior to all others. Your nation is only relevant if you're watching an international sporting event.

The term for this is *campanilismo*, from the word *campanile*, which means belltower, and it refers to your loyalty to the area that you can see from the top of your local belltower. Italians enjoy perpetuating ancient rivalries, such as that between Siena and Florence, or between Rome and Milan. They can tell where someone originates from his dialect and from his attitudes to food, sex and work, and they spend much time analysing whether people are 'typical' of their home towns.

The broadest form of *campanilismo* these days is between north and south. The northerners (called *polentoni*, or polenta eaters, by the southerners) label the southerners lazy and dishonest. The southerners (called *terroni*, or peasants, by the

THE 100 THINGS ...

northerners) label the northerners snobbish, selfish and slow-witted.

The next 12 chapters examine the many different countries within the land called Italy.

WONDERS

75 regions

*h*ere's a summary of Italy's 20 regions, starting at the top left, with a rating out of ten for the degree to which you need to visit each one . . .

☆ **VALLE D'AOSTA.** Capital: Aosta. French is an official language here and Swiss is the feeling. The mountain scenery is spectacular. Main industries: agriculture, iron mining, tourism. Must sees: Gran Paradiso national park, with waterfalls, cliff views and wild ibex, marmots and ermines; the Marmolada mountains; the Pordoi Pass; Aosta's Roman theatre; and the ski resorts at Val Gardena and Cortina d'Ampezzo. Food: fondue or polenta made with fontina cheese. **Rating:** 5 (unless you're a skier, in which case it's 8).

☆ **PIEMONTE.** Capital: Torino (Turin). It's where the notion of an Italy united under the Royal family of Savoy was conceived, and, a century later, where the Red Brigade terrorists got started. Industries: rice growing, dairy cattle, car making (Turin is HQ of Fiat). Must sees: Turin's Automobile Museum (400 models) and Egyptology Museum; the Shroud of Turin in Duomo San Giovanni (but you can only see its urn and photos); Sacra di San Michele monastery (the inspiration for *The Name of the Rose*) near Avigliana. Foods: risotto; white truffles from Alba; *bagna cauda* (warm sauce of olive oil, garlic, anchovies into which raw vegetables are dipped); *agnolotti* (rings stuffed with minced meat); *bollito misto* (mixed spiced meats, with dipping sauces). Wines: Asti Spumante, Barolo, Barbaresco, Nebbiolo, Vermouth (white wine with herbs to make it bitter). **Rating:** 7.

☆ **LOMBARDIA**. Capital: Milano. It's the richest and busiest region. Industries: fashion, steel making, silk, chemicals, banking. Must sees: Lakes Garda, Como, and Maggiore; Certosa di Pavia (a 15th century Carthusian monastery); the ducal palace at Mantua; the upper town of Bergamo; see chapter 81. Foods: gorgonzola, mascarpone and tallegio cheese; *costoletta alla Milanese* (Wiener schnitzel); *osso buco*; *risotto*; *scaloppine*. Wines: Sassella and Inferno (reds), and Campari (made in Milan since 1867). **Rating:** 8.

☆ **TRENTINO-ALTO ADIGE**. Capital: Trento (although the German-speakers will tell you it's really Bolzano). German is an official language here and the style is Austrian (it became an Italian territory only in 1919). Industries: skiing, tourism, agriculture. Must sees: the

Brenta Massif (part of the Dolomite mountains); Brenner Pass. Foods: strudel; gulasch. **Rating**: 4.

☆ **VENETO**. Capital: Venezia. The region is an odd mix of polluting factories and Renaissance glories. Industries: oil refining, chemicals, agriculture. Must sees: Palladio's villas around Vicenza; Roman amphitheatre in Verona; Giotto's frescoes in the Scrovegni chapel at Padua; the wooden bridge at Bassano del Grappa; see chapter 83. Foods: *risi e bisi* (rice and pea stew); *risotto nero* (rice with squid ink); *fegato alla Veneziana* (liver and onions); *brodetto* (fish soup); radicchio (red lettuce). Wines: Soave, Prosecco, Breganze (whites), Bardolino, Valpolicella (reds). **Rating**: 10.

☆ **FRIULI-VENEZIA GIULIA**. Capital: Trieste. It's on the edge of Yugoslavia and guards its independence. Industries: shipbuilding, silk, agriculture. Must sees: the Grotta Gigante, world's largest accessible cave, near Trieste; Piazza della Liberta in Udine; the basilica in Aquileia. Foods: stews with paprika; *cevapcici* (spicy sausage). Wines: Merlot, Pinot grigio. **Rating**: 4.

☆ **LIGURIA**. Capital: Genoa. The coastline starts on the French border and covers the Riviera di Ponente before Genoa and the Riviera di Levante after Genoa. Industries: Fishing, flowers, olives, shipyards. Must sees: Genoa's

THE 100 THINGS ...

old town; the Cinqueterre, a bunch of multicoloured fishing villages; the Portofino Peninsula, especially Chiappa Point; Santa Margarita Lighure. Foods: ravioli; pesto (basil sauce); *sbirra* (tripe soup); *burrida* (fish stew). Wines: Vermentino (white), Dolceaqua (light red). **Rating**: 6.

☆ **EMILIA-ROMAGNA**. Capital: Bologna. It has the best soil in Italy for growing wheat and feeding dairy cattle, hence its emphasis on rich foods. Industries: agriculture, Ferrari cars (Modena), steel making, holidays (Rimini). Must sees: the mosaics of Ravenna, particularly the tomb of Galla Placidia; Ferrara cathedral; see chapter 86. Foods: prosciutto (from Langhirano, near Parma); Parmesan cheese (from Reggio); mortadella sausage; involtini (rolled veal stuffed with spiced mince); tortellini, lasagna and tagliatelle. Wines: Lambrusco (pink), Sangiovese (red), Bertinoro (white from Albana). **Rating**: 7.

☆ **TOSCANA**. Capital: Florence. A tourist-stuffed nightmare in spring, summer and autumn. Industries: agriculture, marble-mining. Must sees: the violent horse race called the Palio delle Contrade in Siena's main square (held on 2 July and 16 August); Piazza dei Miracoli (including the leaning tower) in Pisa; the medieval towers of San Gimignano; see chapters 76 and 84. Foods: *bistecca alla* *fiorentina* (T-bone steak); *zuppa di fagioli* (white bean stew); *pollo alla diavola* (barbecued chicken with crushed pepper); *pappardelle alla lepre* (wide pasta strips with hare stew). Wines: vernaccia (white), and the classic reds Chianti, Tignanello, Brunello di Montalcino, Montepulciano. **Rating**: 9.

☆ **UMBRIA**. Capital: Perugia. The unspoiled answer to Tuscany. Industries: steel making, agriculture. Must sees: the St Francis basilica in Assisi (badly damaged in 1997 earthquake); the well and the cathedral in Orvieto; the old town and the archeological diggings at Gubbio; the ramparts of Montefalco; the food shops of Norcia; see chapter 77. Food: *porchetta* (roast suckling pig); sausages; black truffles. Wines: Orvieto. **Rating**: 8.

☆ **LE MARCHE**. Capital: Ancona. Its Adriatic coastline is crammed with resorts where Italians take their holidays, its interior is fairly untouched. Industries: musical instruments, agriculture, tourism. Must sees: Urbino's ducal palace; the medieval quarter of Ascoli Piceno; Loreto religious sanctuary; the medieval hill town called Sarnano. Foods: *vincisgrassi* (lasagne), roast lamb, *porchetta*, *brodetto* (fish stew with saffron). Wines: Verdicchio (white); Rosso Piceno, Rosso Conero. **Rating**: 5.

☆ **LAZIO**. Capital: Rome. Don't get dazzled by Rome and miss the fascinating countryside

THE 100 THINGS...

around it. Industries: the public service; the Catholic church; agriculture. Must sees: Hadrian's villa and Villa d'Este at Tivoli; the Roman ruins at Ostia Antica; the Etruscan tombs at Tarquinia and Cerveteri; the islands off Anzio; the abbey at Grotaferrata; see chapter 82. Foods: *abbacchio* (roast spring lamb); *saltimbocca* (veal, ham simmered in marsala); *coda alla vaccinara* (oxtail stew); *gnocchi* (made with semolina); *zuppa d'Arzilla* (stew of muddy fish from the Tiber mouth). Wines: Frascati, Falerno, Est! Est! Est! (whites). **Rating**: 9.

☆ **ABRUZZO**. Capital: l'Aquila. This is rugged mountainous country. Industries: car making, steel. Must sees: the basilica of San Bernadino at l'Aquila; Abruzzi national park; the Gran Sasso ski resort; the hotel at Campo Imperatore where Mussolini was imprisoned and then rescued by German paratroopers. Foods: *torrone* (honey and almond nougat); *maccheroni alla chitarra* (pasta cut with strings); roast lamb. Wines: Montepulciano d'Abruzzo, Cerasuola rosé. **Rating**: 5.

☆ **MOLISE**. Capital: Campobasso. This is hillbilly territory, too poor even to have its own mafia. Industries: agriculture. Must sees: the beach at Termoli. Foods: roast lamb; soups. **Rating**: 3.

☆ **CAMPANIA**. Capital: Naples. The crescent around the Bay of Naples is massively

WONDERS

overdeveloped. Industries: oil refining, tobacco growing, agriculture. Must sees: Pompeii; Herculaneum; Capri; Amalfi; Positano; Ravello; see chapter 85. Foods: pizza; *maccheroni*; *zuppa alla marinara* (seafood stew); *capozella* (lamb's head); *insalata caprese* (tomatoes, mozzarella cheese, basil leaves, oil). Wines: Lacryma Christi (white from the slopes of Vesuvius); Capri (white); Gragnano and Taurasi (red). **Rating**: 8.

☆ PUGLIA. Capital: Bari. The heel of the boot is the most sophisticated part of the south after Naples. Industries: wheat, olives. Must sees: the basilica of St Nicholas (Santa Claus) in Bari's old town; the beehive houses called *trulli* around Alberobello. Foods: offal; *orecchiette con ragu* (pasta shaped like little ears, with meat sauce); fish soup; eels. **Rating**: 6.

☆ BASILICATA. Capital: Potenza. This is what they mean when they talk about the poverty of the south. Must sees: 7,000 year old caves, some still inhabited, dug out of the cliff face in Matera. Food: *capretto* (kid stuffed with herbs); bean and chicory soup; spaghetti with anchovies and egg; pasta seasoned with chillis, pimentos and ginger. Wines: Aglianico del Vulture (high alcohol pink). **Rating**: 4.

☆ CALABRIA. Capital: Catanzaro. This is mountainous country, ideal for hiding the kidnapping victims of the local *'ndrangheta*.

THE 100 THINGS ...

Industries: citrus and olive growing. Must sees: the bronze Riace Warriors in the museum of Reggio di Calabria; the Greek ruins at Locri Epizefiri. Foods: forest mushrooms; pork sausages; swordfish; *morseddu* (pig innards and tomato sauce on a kind of pizza). Wines: Ciro (red). **Rating:** 5.

☆ **SICILIA**. Capital: Palermo. The Mafia only kills travellers by accident. Industries: agriculture (citrus, olives, wheat). Must sees: the valley of the temples at Agrigento; Etna volcano; the cathedral at Monreale; the Cappucine catacombs with 8,000 skeletons in Palermo; see chapter 78. Food: cassata (ice cream cake); cous cous with seafood; pasta *con le sarde* (sardines, fennel and pine nuts); swordfish. Wines: Marsala (sherry), red and white Corvo. **Rating:** 8.

☆ **SARDEGNA**. Capital: Cagliari. The inland population is mostly shepherds speaking a language like Catalan. Industries: agriculture. Must sees: Neptune's Cave at Porto Conte; the *nuraghi* (fortresses) near Barumini; the coast road between Arbatax and Dorgali. Foods: pecorino cheese; smoked ham from wild boar; *succutundu* (semolina dumplings in meat sauce). **Rating:** 6.

WONDERS

76
Tuscany

Toscana is a problem. Yes, its olive green hillsides and Siena-red buildings seem perfectly designed to soothe the eye. Yes, it has ancient churches, museums and villas. Yes, with a lot of searching, you can find a decent meal and a great red wine. Yes, it was the cradle of the Renaissance. But for most of the year, Tuscany is a million Anglo-Saxons in search of an Italian.

In the 18th century, the English decided Tuscany symbolised all the things England was not—warm, sensuous, colourful, and happy. But 200 years of foreigners demanding a Room With A View have taken their toll. Nowadays, Tuscany's coastline is so polluted that much of its seafood comes frozen from Asia. Its principal city, Florence, is tired and irritable. Its most famous villages are empty of all but tourist operatives. Its roads are jammed with buses and Porsches. Its surviving culinary speciality—T-bone steak—is the kind of diet we Australians left behind two decades ago.

What is the answer to this? Go to Tuscany in winter, and even then, don't try to stay in Florence or Siena. My suggestion for a base is Lucca, a red Renaissance town about an hour west of Florence by train. Lucca is famous for having the best preserved walls of any Italian town, and for its olive oil, its white beans, the house where Puccini was born, a Roman amphitheatre where medieval houses have replaced the grandstands, and a wooden statue of an angry-looking man on a cross, called The Holy Face of Lucca.

The statue floated ashore in an otherwise empty boat in the 8th century and was thought to have been a carving of Christ done by someone who knew him, using wood from the original cross. William the Conqueror and other French kings used to swear by the Holy Face (*Volto Santo*) and these days the Luccans dress the statue in royal robes and jewellery and parade it through the streets on 13 September every year. The rest of the year it rests in its own little house within San Martino Cathedral.

After you've seen The Face, and solved the maze carved into the cathedral's front wall, you can take a four-kilometre stroll around the top of the walls, which are wide enough in places to contain playgrounds, orchards and sculpture gardens.

The most interesting place to eat in Lucca is Giglio, near Piazza Napoleone, where you should try to sit near the carved marble fireplace and order the *farro* (a brown bean soup made with an ancient grain called spelt), the rabbit and olive stew, or the *bollito misto*. A convenient and attractive place to stay is Piccolo Hotel Puccini (05 855 5421).

It's best to hire a car in Lucca and take a day trip to the north, because there's no other way to get one of Italy's most dizzying experiences: standing on the spot where Michelangelo chose the blocks from which he carved his sculptures, and looking down into a pit that supposedly inspired Dante to write his vision of Hell in *The Divine Comedy*.

This is the Fantiscritti quarry, in the middle of a part of Tuscany called Carrara, a mountain range that supplies the world's finest marble. From a distance these mountains look snow-capped and lopsided. When you get closer, you discover the whiteness is not snow—it's veins of pure marble, and 2,000 years of being chopped up for temples, arches and sculptures have given some of the peaks a very odd shape. The Fantiscritti was first mined by the ancient Romans, who forced slaves to drag blocks weighing many tonnes up sheer cliff faces.

By the time Dante was riding around this neighbourhood (around 1300), the mountains were punctured everywhere by pits with walls of many colours, and it's easy to see how he might visualise a descent into nightmare. (He is supposed to have visited the Malaspina Castle at Fosdinovo, and these days you can climb to a tower room, marked with Dante's bust, where he supposedly slept).

When Michelangelo arrived (around 1515), the process of marble extraction was still claiming hundreds of lives a year, but Michelangelo designed a series of roadways to make it a little easier to get the blocks out of the mountains. Nowadays the marble miners make the descent to the digging spots in a rickety cage, and carve out the blocks with steel wire coated with diamond dust. The blocks are then brought up by machinery rather than slaves, and each year 800,000 tonnes of them are shipped from the port at nearby Marina di Carrara, to make floors, staircases and walls for the world.

A few of the blocks are retained in the town of Carrara and sculptors come from around the world to study at the local academy (set up in 1769) and to carve statues in barn-like structures throughout the town. As you walk round, you're likely to bump into all sorts of gods, heroes, and madonnas, twice life-size and left unfinished by budding sculptors who decided they were not yet up to Michelangelo's standard. You could take them home if you could figure a way to transport them.

For such a spectacular spot, Carrara is surprisingly unvisited by the tourists who infest the rest of Tuscany. Maybe they've heard that the area historically has been the heart of the Italian anarchist movement, and they're expecting bombs to be thrown at them. Maybe they think the drive, via steep, narrow, winding roads, is too difficult. But the drive repays the effort with much more than quarries. On top of most of these mountains are grim castles built in the 14th century by the various warring families of the region.

WONDERS

At the opposite end of the marble coast from Lucca there's another sensational restaurant. It's called Ciccio, at Bocca di Magra near La Spezia (01 876 5568). In this sprawling bungalow on the bank of the Magra River, fresh seafood is not so much a speciality as an obsession. Its version of farro soup contains baby octopus as well as spelt grains. Its spaghetti has an intense sauce of *bottarga* (tuna roe). Its antipasto is a creature of infinite variety, including tiny squid fried with a bit of chilli, mussels stuffed with spinach paste, smoked tuna with rocket, fish pickled in apple vinegar, baked scampi with olives, and prawns with artichokes.

It's easy to reach this part of Tuscany without going anywhere near Florence: just land at Pisa airport (daily connections to London) and take the half-hour train ride from the airport to Lucca. You can make day trips to all the region's major sites if you feel compelled to tick them off. If you're leaving via Pisa airport, allow an extra hour before your flight to see the Piazza dei Miracoli, which contains the Leaning Tower. It's a ten-minute cab ride from the airport.

77
Umbria

*U*mbria is now what Tuscany was 70 years ago, which means starting to be sophisticated without being spoiled. It was lucky enough to get the railways much later than Tuscany, and until the 20th century, its only tourists were pilgrims in search of Saint Francis.

While Tuscany has hill towns, Umbria has mountain citadels. While Tuscany shows off the glories of the Renaissance and the Roman Empire, Umbria preserves the austerity of the Middle Ages and the Etruscan Empire that preceded Rome. While Tuscany microwaves frozen seafood, Umbria grills sausages made from wild pigs that have fed on acorns in the forest, seasoned with black truffles.

Umbria has a lot of weird stuff. In Assisi you can gaze at the 700 year old mummified corpse of Saint Clare in the Santa Chiara church, as well as Clare's grey curls in a glass box and her lacy nightie in a display case, next to a tattered robe once worn by Saint Francis. The locals reckon Clare and Francis had an affair sometime around the year 1210. Not that there's anything wrong with that, they say— celibacy was not required of the religious in the

WONDERS

13th century. In Umbria, some gossip is good enough to last 700 years.

On top of the mountain behind the town of Gubbio, there's a basilica which contains the brown-skinned mummy of Saint Ubaldo, who fought off various barbarians in 1155. In the basilica you can also see the three *ceri*, which are four-metre-tall wooden pillars used in the annual festival of Ubaldo. On 15 May each year, huge wax figures of saints Ubaldo, Anthony and George are mounted on top of these pillars, and the totem poles thus created are carried through the streets of Gubbio and up the hill in a race between teams dedicated to each saint.

Once you've seen the mummy and the *ceri*, you can wander across to the archeological diggings, which regularly unearth relics of the Umbri tribe that lived on these hills in the 4th century BC. The Umbri were a placid lot in a period when all the other tribes were warmongers, yet somehow the Umbri managed to persuade the Etruscans not to tear them apart. The image of Umbria as the most peaceful and reflective region of Italy may have grown from this ancient reputation, and certainly Gubbio is famed these days for its quietness.

If you take the rattly little funicular back down the hill to Gubbio, you can gaze on evidence of the Umbri tribe in the Consuls' Palace, a 14th century fortress which now guards a set of bronze plates called the Eugubian tablets, a history of pre-Christian times written in Etruscan, Latin and Umbrian.

Satisfied with your scholarship, you can move on to dinner at the Taverna del Lupo (tavern of the wolf). It's named after a miracle performed by Francis of Assisi when he made a special guest appearance at Gubbio in 1220. Having honed his animal-communication skills with the birds of Assisi, he was able to persuade a wolf to stop attacking the townsfolk of Gubbio. Taverna del Lupo serves a wonderful soup called *imbrecciata*, thick with beans, corn, lentils, peas and celery. The menu says it's from a 'Eugubian' recipe, which presumably means it was eaten by the ancient Romans when the town was called Iguvium. It's unlikely that back then the soup included corn, which only arrived in Italy in the 16th century, after Columbus found it in South America. But no-one's complaining.

The wierdness continues in Orvieto, where I swear there's an emu sticking out of the facade of the cathedral. How a sculptor of gargoyles in the early 14th century could ever have seen an emu is a mystery worthy of *The X-Files*, but it's only a tiny part of the wonders of that cathedral, which is zebra-striped in alternate layers of black and white marble and covered with gorgeous mosaics and balconies. It was built (between 1190 and 1600) to house the relics of an 11th century event called 'the miracle at Bolsena'—some biscuits which began to bleed, thereby proving, by the logic of the time, that they were the body of Jesus. Under the organ there is the 'corporal chapel', where the cloth that wrapped the bleeding biscuits is kept in a gold reliquary encrusted with jewels.

Orvieto sits on top of a plug of rock thrust out of the ground by an ancient volcano. You can spend many pleasant hours getting lost in the medieval maze of tiny lanes winding between terracotta-roofed houses made of the same brown volcanic rock.

And there's a strange well, built in the 1530s at the order of Pope Clement the Seventh, who had taken refuge behind Orvieto's high walls after French troops sacked Rome, and who wanted to guarantee a water supply. The Pozzo di San Patrizio project turned into a miracle of engineering, with two spiral staircases, each of 248 steps, winding around the shaft but never meeting. Undertaking the downward climb and the upward return leaves you with trembling thighs and a sense that you've earned another glass of the local white wine made from grapes grown in the volcanic soil (the dry version being a lot better than the sweet *abbocato* version). The place to consume it is a local restaurant called Trattoria La Grotta, which specialises in pork, beef and seasonal vegetable dishes, often flavoured with truffles.

But if truffles are your passion, you have to venture further east into the least-visited wilds of

Umbria. In fact, you'll have to hire a car—while Assisi, Gubbio and Orvieto are all on the train line, the gourmet capital of the region, Norcia, is not. Drive into the mountains and you'll find an area where sheep feed on wild thyme and sage and where pigs feed on acorns and truffles in the forest.

The meat of Norcia is so fine that in Rome, the word for a pork butcher is 'Norcineria'. The streets of Norcia are lined with food shops where sausages and pheasants hang from the rafters and cheeses and wild mushrooms spill from the counters. Visit Norcia in November, and you'll find yourself in the middle of a truffle festival. If you're inclined to think black truffles taste like cardboard, Norcia will change your mind—especially if you're staying and eating at the Hotel-ristorante Granaro del Monte, where the Bianconi family have been truffle fanatics since 1800.

If you're fancying a little fish by this point in your meaty pilgrimage, Umbria can oblige this craving too. Although it has no sea coast, Umbria has one of Italy's largest and least polluted lakes—Trasimeno, which is not far from the region's capital, Perugia. Trasimeno is best known as the spot where, on 24 June, 217 BC, the Carthaginian general Hannibal wiped out the Roman army under Flaminius. But modern foodies know it better as the source of eels, carp, perch, trout and pike, which are often served together in a local stew called *tegamaccio*.

About half an hour's drive from Trasimeno is the town of Torgiano, which contains an amazing hotel-restaurant called Tre Vaselle. Its owners make a dry white called Torre di Giano and have set up a wine museum which proves that travellers have been drinking well in the region since Etruscan times. It's the perfect place to sit back and contemplate Umbria's simple superiority in all the experiences that matter.

WONDERS

78
Sicily

*i*f Umbria is how Tuscany was 70 years ago, then Sicily is how Umbria must have been 150 years ago. Sicilians just don't seem to care about encouraging tourism, though it could be a useful source of income for an impoverished island. Perhaps they have something else on their minds.

This lack of self-consciousness can be pleasant for the traveller who wants to peacefully peel back the layers left by invading Phoenicians, Greeks, Romans, Arabs, Normans, French, and Spanish, but the downside is that you can't see Sicily quickly. If you're planning an anti-clockwise circuit from Palermo to Taormina, which is the logical way to cover the place, you need to allow about seven days, of which a total of three will be spent getting lost. Sicilians don't bother much with signposts, because they know where they're going, and they haven't yet realised that strangers might want to find something in particular.

Palermo was seriously damaged during World War II, and much of it has not yet been repaired. The three big squares in the middle—Quattro Canti, with its baroque facades, Piazza Pretoria, with its marble fountain, and Piazza Bellini, with Moorish

WONDERS

and Norman facades—give a hint of how grand the town could be if anybody cared. Its food market, the Vucciria, shows how much wealth Sicily can still produce from its soil and its sea.

On a hill just out of town is the village of Monreale, with a wonderful 13th century Norman cathedral with Moorish decorations, mosaics and delicate cloisters. Two hours' drive to the southwest is Segesta, a massive limestone temple that almost leaves the Parthenon in the shade. It stands on a hill in the middle of nowhere, and nobody knows why it was built (around 400 BC).

The most inspiring survivors of the Greek period are near the town of Agrigento. If you stay in a hotel called the Villa Athena, you can see them from your balcony and reach them simply by walking through the hotel's olive grove and hopping over a stone fence. There's a row of nine temples built around 450 BC, and a massive fallen statue (seven metres long) that looks like a sunbaking giant. The Temple of Olympian Zeus is the biggest in the world (113 metres long by 54 metres wide), but most of it has collapsed. The golden Temple of Concord is the best preserved in Sicily (because it was used as a Christian Church till the 18th century) and at sunset on Saturdays it's the favorite spot in Agrigento for the taking of wedding photos.

Sicily also does a nice line in pretty towns with no visible populations. The quaintest is Erice, which

THE 100 THINGS . . .

should be in France instead of on a clifftop on the west coast of Sicily. Narrow cobbled streets apparently used only by cats lead up to a spectacular castle built by the Normans in the 14th century out of stones pinched from a Greek temple on the same spot. The most sinister in its silence is Corleone, from which the most savage faction of the mafia spread to take control of the entire organisation during the 1980s.

Near another Norman town, Piazza Armerina, archeologists in the 1950s uncovered a Roman villa from the 3rd century AD with the most beautiful mosaic floors in the world. You can walk over bridges of scaffolding and look down at 40 scenes of recreations enjoyed 1600 years ago. There are chariot races, girls in bikinis playing volley ball, children chasing rabbits and ducks, adults hunting lions and tigers which are now extinct, cherubs riding seaserpents, and lots and lots of feasting.

After the silence of those places, Taormina comes as a shock. A 20-minute drive up a series of hairpin bends is followed by a half-hour search for a parking spot, because Taormina is buried under tourists, most of whom seem to be German. Cars are banned from the main street, Corso Umberto, but that doesn't prevent you from being knocked over by backpacks. There are sensational views, particularly the sight of Mount Etna through the columns of the Roman Theatre, if you can see them between the bodies.

WONDERS

We should be grateful to Taormina for attracting all the tourists who might otherwise clutter up Syracuse, which is easy to walk around despite being Sicily's liveliest town, a title it has held since 500 BC, when it became the Manhattan of the Mediterranean.

The adjoining island of Ortygia, crammed with 2000 years of structures, needs a day's exploring. The nearby Greek Theatre and Paradise Quarry are must sees, especially the grotto called The Ear of Dionysius where a tyrant (around 380 BC) supposedly used to listen to the amplified conversations of people he had imprisoned below.

Siracusa deserves a couple of nights' stay. The Hotel Villa Politi is a model of faded grandeur and ornate gardens. It was once the favourite holiday spot of Winston Churchill, and it's moderately priced because not much of it has been renovated lately. People allergic to mould might prefer the thoroughly reconstructed Grand Hotel on Ortygia. Restaurants such as Rossini and Arlecchino offer interesting seafood dishes that break out of the *Pasta Con le Sarde* rut which afflicts much of Sicily.

WONDERS

79
the other islands

Sicily and Sardinia are Italy's biggest islands, but here's a bunch of others you really ought to float away to ...

☆ **CAPRI** (by ferry from the Mergellina dock in Naples or from Sorrento). Nearly 2,000 years of tourist exploitation, from the time when it was the holiday hideaway of the emperor Tiberius, has not spoiled Capri's beauty. Once you get away from the crowds in Piazza Umberto, you can find isolation on the walk to Tiberius's Villa Jovis, and on the chairlifts to Anacapri and Monte Solaro. You could pay a fortune for a boat ride into the Blue Grotto, or you could swim into it when the boats aren't running—before 9 a.m. and after 6 p.m.

☆ **ISCHIA** (by ferry from Naples or Sorrento). Less posh than Capri but still overrun by Germans, its attractions are beaches, hot springs, the view from Monte Epomeo and the ruins of Castello d'Ischia (which include the Museum of Instruments of Torture and Capital Punishment).

☆ **ELBA** (by ferry from Piombino Maritimo on

WONDERS

the Tuscan coast near Grossetto). Famed as the place of exile for Napoleon, and before that for its iron deposits, its attractions are clean beaches, the Napoleon museum and villa, and the view from Monte Capanne.

☆ **The EGADI** islands (by hydrofoil from Trapani on the west coast of Sicily). Levanzo and Marettimo are wild and interesting, with signs of ancient dwellings and prehistoric cave art, while Favignana is commercialised.

☆ **The EOLIE** (or **Lipari**) islands (by hydrofoil from Milazzo, northern Sicily, or from Messina). There are seven of them, of which the most interesting are **Stromboli** for its active volcano and its Malvasia wine; **Vulcano** for its four volcanoes, its sulphur springs, and its Great Crater; and **Lipari**, for its Norman-Spanish castle and its dishes made with local capers and Malvasia.

☆ **The TREMITI** islands (by hydrofoil from Termoli on the west coast of Abruzzo). San Nicola has an 11th century abbey and San Domino has pine forests.

☆ **The BORROMEO** islands in Lake Maggiore (by ferry from Stresa). The most famous is Isola Bella, with its wedding cake Baroque palace and white peacocks, but Isola Madre has an amazing botanical garden and doll museum, while Isola dei Pescatori is a bunch of souvenir stalls.

THE 100 THINGS ...

☆ **The PONZIANE** (Pontine) islands (by ferry from Anzio on the west coast of Lazio). **Ponza** is a weekend playground for Romans, known for its seafood, lentil soup, beaches and brightly painted houses, while **Ventotene** is a peaceful refuge.

WONDERS

80
the other countries

*i*nside Italy are three independent nations, two not much more than gimmicks and one immensely wealthy ...

☆ **THE REPUBLIC OF SAN MARINO** is a 26 square kilometre city-state, inhabited by 26,000 people, not far from Rimini. It's a pretty cobbled hill town with a fake-looking white castle and panoramic views from three towers. It survives by selling its own coins, stamps and trinkets.

☆ **THE KNIGHTS OF MALTA**, a Catholic order founded in Jerusalem in 1048, technically run a nation of their own (with 10,000 citizens) in various locations in Rome, issuing their own coins and stamps, although they have no territory.

☆ **THE VATICAN** was a vast owner of land around Rome for 1,000 years before it was taken over by the new Italian government in 1870. In 1929, it became its own country again when the Pope reached an agreement with Mussolini, but nowadays it covers less than a square kilometre within walls adjoining St Peter's. The city-state has 1,000 inhabitants, its own coins, flag, anthem, and legal system. Its postal service is far more efficient than Italy's, and worth using if you want your postcards to reach home before you do.

WONDERS

81
Milan

Napoleon made Milan the capital of Italy in 1805, and the two million Milanese think that should still be the case, since they make the most money and pay the most taxes (even if Rome has a bigger population). In fact, Milan could make a plausible case for being the capital of Europe. It may not have as many tourist sites as the cities to the south, but it's where the action is in design, fashion, politics, banking and food. Get ready to spend.

Must sees: La Scala opera house; Peck food stores; the roof of the Duomo (Italy's greatest gothic cathedral); the shopping streets and the night life around Piazza San Babila; Castello Sforzesco, the former home of the dukes of Milan, now a bunch of museums; the Brera art gallery, with works by all the Renaissance heavies; the railway station (Fascist massiveness); Da Vinci's *Last Supper* in the refectory (*cenacolo*) of the Santa Maria delle Grazie church; the Da Vinci Museum of Science and Technology.

Eating suggestions: Bistro di Gualtiero Marchesi, on top of Rinascente department store with a view of the Duomo roof; Peck's restaurant; Aimo e

THE 100 THINGS . . .

Nadia, small, friendly, adventurous but expensive and out of the city centre.

Staying suggestions: Spadari al Duomo, with the latest in groovy local design; Antica Locanda Solferino, for 19th century quaintness and 20th century plumbing.

Day trips: the Gothic *Certosa* (monastery) at Pavia.

WONDERS

82
Rome

*f*ounded on 21 April, 754 BC, Roma has been undergoing expensive renovations in recent years, designed to make it beautiful for 2000, which has been declared a jubilee year for reasons not entirely clear. The pall of pollution has lightened as restrictions on inner-city traffic seem to be triumphing over the Roman knack of avoiding inconvenient laws. Much of it now makes very pleasant walking, without the population pressure of Florence, the preciousness of Venice or the pomposity of Milan.

Must sees: the Colosseum (*Colosseo*); the Forum (*Foro Romano*); the Pantheon; the Capitol Hill (*Campidoglio*); the Sistine Chapel (*Cappella Sistina*); St Paul's Outside The Walls (*San Paolo Fuori le Mura*); Piazza Navona; Trevi Fountain; the Spanish Steps (*Piazza di Spagna*); Campo de Fiori.

Eating suggestions: Checchino, in Monte Testaccio near the old abbattoir district (but only if you love meat and fine wine); Da

Giggetto, in the old Ghetto, for Jewish food and fried artichokes; Alberto Ciarla in Trastevere.

Staying suggestions: La Residenza, comfortable, medium priced and near the Spanish Steps; Hotel Nerva, near the Forum, with ancient beams but modern plumbing; Teatro di Pompeo, on the spot where Caesar was stabbed, near the Campo de Fiori.

Day trips: Hadrian's Villa at Tivoli, Ostia Antica, Frascati and the nearby hill towns.

WONDERS

83
Venice

*g*et used to the idea that Venice is not a real place—it's an open air museum. Travellers who seek 'the spots where the locals gather' are engaging in an academic exercise, since the indigenous population of Venice dropped from 200,000 in the early 1960s to 60,000 in the mid 1990s. If you want non-tourist nightlife and 'real' restaurants, you need to cross the bridge back to the mainland and eat in a place like Trattoria dall'Amelia in Mestre (the industrial sprawl whose pollution is dissolving the facades of Venice).

But *La Serenissima* is still an essential experience in everyone's life. If you go in winter, you can find serene spots for reflecting on a city on 177 islands that became a trading empire controlling the Adriatic and much of northern Italy in the early 15th century.

You don't need to spend $80 on a gondola ride. You can get the same effect by spending $1 on a *traghetto* across the Grand Canal. And it's possible to eat well if you stay away from St Mark's Square and any place with a menu in four languages.

Must sees: the Rialto bridge (and the early morning fish market next to it on the left bank);

San Marco basilica; Doge's Palace (Palazzo Ducale) with the Bridge of Sighs (Ponte dei Sospiri) and Casanova's cell; the Ghetto; the residential district near the public gardens; and the art museums called Accademia (lots of Bellinis) and Scuola di San Rocco (Tintorettos).

Eating suggestions: Ristorante Antiche Carampane in San Polo district, which does great seafood and has a sign outside saying 'No pizza. No lasagne. No menu turistico'; Trattoria Anzolo Raffael in Dorsoduro, plain and tiny with no frills freshness.

Staying suggestions: Hotel La Fenice et les Artistes, near St Mark's, for a quaintly operatic atmosphere at medium prices; La Favretti, near the Rialto, for a 15th century mini-palace at modest prices.

Day trips out of town: Treviso, Vicenca, Verona.

WONDERS

84
Florence

*t*here will be a queue for the Uffizi gallery. There will be a queue for Michelangelo's David in the Galleria dell'Accademia (the real statue, not the reproduction in the Piazza della Signoria) and you'll get ten minutes to see all the Michelangelos before you're shuffled out. The shopkeepers will be impatient. The restaurants will serve boring food. That's just the way it is for most of the year in Firenze, city of the Renaissance geniuses.

Must sees: the Ponte Vecchio (the bridge where Dante allegedly spotted Beatrice); the Duomo (technically the Cathedral of Santa Maria del Fiore) with Brunelleschi's dome; the Bargello palace (formerly the police chief's home, now a sculpture museum); the Palazzo Vecchio (where the Medici lived).

Eating suggestions: Cibreo, expensive but exciting, and its attached trattoria is cheaper; Trattoria Garga, with adventurous combinations; Cantinetta Antinori, with okay food and lots of wines by the glass.

Staying suggestions: Hotel Malaspina, old building, new renovation, just north of the Duomo; Hermitage Hotel, which has quaint rooms with a view of the Arno.

WONDERS

85
Naples

Some travellers avoid Napoli because they've read about the air pollution, pickpocketing, heavy traffic, uncollected rubbish and unemployment. In fact, the phrase 'See Naples and die' was never a reference to the crime rate, but a 19th century comment on the city's beauty and energy—both of which are still just as impressive. During the 1990s, an enlightened mayor named Antonio Bassolino has done much to clean up the city on the bay, and travellers who stay with the crowds have no more to fear than in any seaport.

Must sees: the port of Santa Lucia; Spacca Napoli (the old town, around Via Benedetto Croce and S. Biagio dei Librai); the National Archeological Museum, especially the artworks recovered from Herculaeneum; the Castel Nuovo (built in 1282); the 18th century Palazzo di Capodimonte, now housing 1000 years of artworks.

Eating suggestions: Don Salvatore, creative seafood and a wide wine list on the seafront at Mergellina; La Cantinella, on a terrace at Santa Lucia, with classic local dishes.

Staying suggestions: Hotel Santa Lucia, with a view of the Bay; Hotel Miramare, a villa and former US consulate, with a roof garden.

Day trips: Capri; Erculano; Vesuvio; Pompeii.

86 Bologna

*I*talians have given Bologna a lot of nicknames: *la dotta* (the learned) because it contains Italy's oldest university and has been a birthplace of great ideas; *la grassa* (the fat), because it eats so well; *la rossa* (the red), originally because of its red roofs but now because over the past 50 years it has kept re-electing the most efficient left-wing city council in the nation. Bologna also has a reputation for being sex-obsessed, and has been regularly condemned by popes for its hedonism. You may find an opportunity to check this allegation.

Must sees: the adjacent squares in the old town centre, Piazza Nettuno and Piazza Maggiore; the twin leaning towers in the Piazza di Porta Ravegnana (and you should climb the Asinelli tower for a panorama of the red roofed city); the basilica of San Petronio, with its unfinished facade; the university, along Via Zamboni; the many kilometres of colonnades.

Eating suggestions: Franco Rossi, specialising

in handmade tortellini in broth with truffles; La Columbina (sausages); and anywhere the wandering chef Silverio Cineri is currently cooking.

Staying suggestions: Hotel al Capello Rosso, near Piazza Maggiore, with a flowery atrium; Hotel Corona d'Oro, in a former palace but medium-priced.

Day trips: San Domenico restaurant at Imola.

WONDERS

87
over and under

*t*his is just an exercise in personal bias, but here's my list of the most overrated places in Italy:

Portofino: pretty facades on buildings that house expensive shops designed to rip off overawed Americans.

Sorrento: mainly a grotty colony for English package tourists, not deserving its glamour-by-association with the Amalfi coast.

San Gimignano: a pleasant medieval town, but there are many in Tuscany and Umbria like it, and they aren't crammed with tour buses.

Taormina: cute, but most of the year not worth the trouble of getting up there and fighting the crowds. (Meanwhile, nearby Tindari, with inspiring Greek and Roman ruins, gets unfairly ignored.)

Florence: unless you're obsessed with art treasures, or go in winter, it's the same problem as Taormina.

Here's my list of the most underrated places in Italy:

Genoa: chopped up by expressways, but much remains that is fascinating from its heroic seafaring past.

Turin: important both historically (the birthplace

of united Italy) and for its modern architecture and car designs.

Naples: too exciting to let yourself be put off by its reputation.

Lecce: a splendidly decorated town in Puglia, that reached a peak in the 17th century and is nicknamed 'the baroque Florence' (without the crowds).

Alberobello: near Bari (in Italy's heel), it displays the extraordinary *trulli*, 500 year old beehive houses and churches.

Places you thought would be overrated but actually live up to their hype: Venice; Capri; the drive from Positano along the Amalfi coast to Ravello.

NATURE

88
disasters

*W*hile Australia specialises in droughts, floods and bushfires, Italy is prone to landslides, mudflows, avalanches, earthquakes, floods and volcanic eruptions. There are also manmade disasters in the form of air pollution emergencies resulting from carbon monoxide and from industrial emissions such as sulphur dioxide, and waterways polluted by industrial and agricultural effluents.

But the biggest disaster has been the extent to which the money allocated by governments for disaster relief has failed to reach the people most afflicted, particularly in the south. In 1980, for example, an earthquake struck Irpinia in Basilicata, killing 3,100 people and leaving 200,000 homeless. Over the next ten years the government supposedly spent 51,000 billion lire repairing the damage. But in 1990, a parliamentary inquiry found that a third of the victims were still living in prefabricated huts. Much of the money had been diverted to the Camorra and to the family of the former Christian Democrat prime minister Ciriaco De Mica.

In 1997, the area around Assisi was hit by earthquakes, which got huge publicity because they

NATURE

damaged parts of the cathedral of St Francis. The Government committed billions of lire to restoration projects, which are unlikely to show much result till next century. The people forced to live in shipping containers because their homes were destroyed have complained of slow progress.

Early in 1998, mudslides resulting from deforestation and illegal building projects on hillsides at Sarno, near Naples, killed 150 people and made more than 1,000 homeless. The Italian media called it 'Pompeii 2000', and ecology experts said some 45 per cent of Italy was in similar danger from mudslides. The government demanded strict police checking on all companies seeking reconstruction contracts, to ensure the Camorra would not benefit from the relief program, but this made the process so slow that the honesty checks had to be abandoned.

PRACTICALITIES

89
weather

*h*ow many times do I have to tell you: don't go in August. Italy is stinking hot and crammed with Americans and Germans, and half the decent eating places are closed for the summer holidays, while the others have doubled their prices. My favourite travelling times are April (early spring) and November (late autumn), but January is exhilarating, especially if you can catch a snowfall in Venice.

The far north gets cold snowy winters and humid summers; the area around the Po valley (north of Bologna across to Verona) gets damp winters and dry summers, with dense fogs in autumn. The south has very hot summers and mild winters.

PRACTICALITIES

Around Milan, July is the wettest month, but temperatures at that time of year can rise to 28 degrees, while January temperatures can sink to freezing point.

Around Florence, October is the wettest month, while July has temperatures as high as 29 degrees and January has temperatures down to two. Around Rome, October is the wettest month, with July temperatures up to 29 and January down to 4.5. And in Sicily, it's moderately rainy from October to January, with a top of 29 in July and a low of 9 in January.

The seasons are strictly observed. Fruits and vegetables are celebrated for their brief availability, and then anticipated for the rest of the year. Italians believe there are certain things you do in each season, and on the date when that season is over, you stop. If you went swimming in September, for example, even if it's very hot, Italians would consider you eccentric, because *la stagione e finita*.

PRACTICALITIES

90
holidays

*t*ravellers in Italy encounter the sign *chiuso per ferie* on the doors of museums and historic sites so often that they tend to develop the theory that Italians are permanently on holidays. In fact, the 10 official *ferie* (public holidays) are ...

1 January: *Capodanno* (New Years Day)

6 January: *La Befana* (Epiphany)

End of March: *Pasquetta* (Easter Monday)

25 April: *Anniversario della Liberazione* (Liberation Day, for the end of World War II)

1 May: *Primo Maggio* (May Day)

15 August: *Ferragosto* (Assumption)

1 November: *Ognissanti* (All Saints Day)

8 December: *L'Immacolata Concezzione* (Immaculate Conception)

25 December: *Natale* (Christmas)

26 December: *Santo Stefano* (Boxing Day—Saint Stephen's Day).

In addition, every town has its own particular feast day dedicated to a local saint, when nobody minds if workers goof off. Oddly, 4 October, the day dedicated to Saint Francis, Italy's national saint, is not a holiday, though some devout folk take it off anyway. There is also some festive activity on

PRACTICALITIES

2 June, which is the anniversary of the founding of the republic in 1946, and on 17 March, the anniversary of the unification of Italy in 1861.

If one of the official holidays falls on a Tuesday or a Thursday, many Italians will take off the adjoining Monday or Friday, as *la ponte* (the bridge) to the weekend.

And of course, most business and government activity closes down between 20 July and 20 August while the workers head for the beach (usually their own coastline—Italians rarely take holidays overseas).

PRACTICALITIES

91
airports

*W*ithin Italy, you'd be insane to get about by plane, when the trains work so well. But arriving from outside the country, or travelling between the peninsula and Sicily or Sardinia, you find the airports are a study in diversity. My favourities are Pisa and Venice, which are small enough to have their own characters.

Pisa airport (which serves all of Tuscany) is only three kilometres from the city centre, so you could take a taxi (something you would not do from most other Italian airports) or, if you don't have much luggage, jump on the local bus (after buying your ticket inside the terminal). Pisa airport is half an hour by train from Lucca and an hour from Florence.

You can take a bus from Venice airport to the edge of the city, but that's hardly getting into the spirit of things. Far better to take the waterbus, which goes every hour from a dock adjoining the terminal, and takes 50 minutes to chug past increasingly inhabited islands until the domes of St Mark's emerge through the mist.

If you're heading for Milan, the airport to avoid is Malpensa, which is an hour by bus from the city. Give your preference to an airline or a flight that will bring you into Linate, which is only 7 km from the centre of town.

For Sicily, my advice is to fly into Palermo airport, hire a car, drive anticlockwise round the island, and fly to the mainland from Catania.

Rome's Leonardo da Vinci airport (also called Fiumicino) is 30 km from the city centre, so rather than spend $40 on a cab, it's best to take the train. The station is a short walk from the arrivals area (look for 'FS' signs). Ask at the train ticket counter for 'Termini', or use the machines on the station, and it should cost you 15,000 L for a ticket. When you reach Termini (Rome's central station) half an hour later, head straight out the front for a taxi to your hotel. Say 'No, grazie' to anyone who approaches you inside the train terminal (or inside any air terminal for that matter) offering a ride to town. The legal cabbies are outside in clearly marked taxis (with meters).

And if you're flying out of Rome late in the evening, think about checking in your luggage at the airport early and then taking a cab over to the seaside village of Fiumicino (ten minutes away) where a meal at Bastianelli al molo will preserve the Italian experience till the last possible moment.

How to make milk froth at altitude

Ladies and gentlemen, kindly remain seated during this turbulence.

PRACTICALITIES

92
hotels

Some Italian hotels are so magnificent that they become destinations in themselves, regardless of their surroundings. As if Venice itself was not enough, the Danieli Hotel, just down from the Doge's Palace, is legendary—a 16th century palace in which Monteverdi's opera *Proserpina Rapita* was first performed in 1630, it became home away from home during the 19th century for the likes of Charles Dickens, Richard Wagner and Marcel Proust. If you don't feel inclined to pay $700 a night to stay in one of the Danieli's suites overlooking the Grand Canal, you should at least walk into it when you visit Venice, check out its lobby and wander up its golden staircase.

Other hotels which deserve similar reverential examination are the Principe di Savoia in Milan, the Eden in Rome, the Baglioni in Bologna, the Excelsior in Florence, the Villa San Michele in Fiesole, the Villa Sassi in Turin, the Vesuvio in Naples and the Villa d'Este at Lake Como. If you're interested in the art of hospitality, you may feel it's worth budgeting to stay one night in one of these gilded dinosaurs, and live on crusts and cockroaches for the rest of your travels.

PRACTICALITIES

Coming back to earth, you need to know that the Italian Government classifies all forms of accommodation on a scale between one and five stars, from cheap and basic to super-luxurious (all the hotels in the previous paragraph have five stars). The rating tells the hotel how much it is allowed to charge.

In my experience, hotels and pensioni with three stars are usually small and helpful, with all the facilities a traveller needs, while four-star places tend to be large, impersonal and pretentious, without the mythical qualities that are supposed to make the five-stars worth their prices.

A model of the ideal three-star is a place called the Pensione Bencista, near Fiesole in the hills overlooking Florence (phone or fax 39 55 59163). It has antique-decorated rooms with bathrooms attached, great views, and interesting meals. And the number 7 bus to Florence stops right outside the door. You pay $250 a night for a double room with dinner included. I assume the reason the Bencista doesn't get a four-star classification is that it doesn't accept credit cards.

A growing trend is what the Italians call *agriturismo*—farmhouses converted into guesthouses. They're ideal for people who don't want to stay in a big city, but the catch is that you need to hire a car to see more than the immediate neighbourhood. An example is Camiano Piccolo (phone or fax 39 742 379492) near the medieval town of Montefalco

THE 100 THINGS ...

in Umbria (30 km from Assisi). It's a 400 year old farmhouse which now has 14 rooms (each with bathroom and a TV set) and a swimming pool. You pay around $200 a night for a double room and an excellent rest.

If you have access to a computer attached to the Internet, you can put 'agritour' in the search space and find loads of options. Or ask a travel agent for a list of farm hotels.

PRACTICALITIES

93
trains

*I*talian trains are fast, efficient and reasonably priced, and if you find one with a dining car, it will serve a good meal with an ever-changing floor show. Your most helpful guide is the Thomas Cook red timetable for Europe (available at Thomas Cook travel agencies). Not only does it tell you what times the trains depart and arrive, but it indicates which ones have dining cars (a crossed knife and fork symbol) and which ones require advance reservations.

There is, however, a small detail: like almost everything else in Italy, trains come attached to a bureaucracy. You may have turned up early at the station to buy your ticket, knowing that you'd have to line up behind a parade of grandmothers arguing with the ticket clerk about their pension discounts. And you may have gone to a separate window to pay the supplement for a seat reservation, and the supplement because the train is superfast, and the supplement because there's a dining car. That might look like the end of the paperwork, but once you are seated, you will be visited by an inspector who will tell you amiably that there's a detail you overlooked. My favourite was the inspector who told me that the *chilometri* pass I had bought in Australia was a fine thing, and I had been quite right to pay a supplement to guarantee a seat, but I still needed to pay him a 10,000 lire 'stamping fee'. When I paid up, he filled out a form in triplicate, gave me a carbon copy, stamped the pass, and then sat down to chat to us for 15 minutes about the area through which the train was passing.

The main categories of Italian trains are:

TEE (Trans-Europe Express) or ***Super Rapido***, which usually has big comfortable seats and a dining car, and which stops only at major cities.

Rapido, which is also fast and likely to skip small stations, but which may not have a dining car.

Espresso, which stops at more towns, but not all of them.

Diretto, which stops almost everywhere.

Accelerato, sometimes called *locale*, which stops at every station along the way, and often between stations for no apparent reason.

Note: the word for strike is *sciopero*. If you see that written on a sign at a railway station, find an inquiries desk where someone speaks English and clarify if it affects today's trains or just some subset of officialdom.

PRACTICALITIES

94
driving

*h*ere are some good reasons not to drive in Italy: petrol is expensive, and so are the fees for using the autostrada; petrol stations are open only eight hours a day, and usually take a break between 12.30 and 2.30 just as you roll into town verging on empty, or have just closed when you roll into town at 7.35 p.m.; you must drive on the right, which can be confusing when you have to make a left turn; Italian drivers enjoy going fast, taking shortcuts, and running yellow lights, and are likely to tailgate cautious foreign drivers.

But you have decided to hire a car anyway, because you want to see the countryside and tiny villages rather than just the places you can reach by train. You should know that the Autostrada del Sole runs down the spine of Italy, and you can get from Rome to Milan on it in five hours. Legally you only need carry your passport and your Australian driver's licence, but it's useful to get an international driver's licence issued by a motorists' organisation such as the NRMA or RACV, because the Italian police are more likely to recognise that as an official document.

The main traffic rule is that you must give way

to cars on your right, unless you're on a priority road (marked with a yellow and white diamond). The speed limit is 130 km/h on autostradas, 110 on four-lane highways, 90 on country roads and 50 in urban areas. Italy has the highest rate of car accidents (*incidente stradale*) in Europe.

PRACTICALITIES

95
getting around town

*i*f you're not in a hurry (and why would you be?), public transport is the way to learn about Italian life. As you sit in the bus or the subway, you can calmly observe the advertisements, the clothes, the attitudes and the gestures of other passengers. If you see something interesting through the window, get off, have a look, and catch the next bus.

Let's use Rome as an example, since its public transport system was a model for other big Italian cities. The same ticket works for the bus or the metro, and you can buy tickets at metro stations (marked with a big M) at some newsstands, and from tobacconists, which are marked with a T sign. You must buy your ticket before you get on the bus, and you have to stick it into the stamping machine as soon as you get on board (otherwise an inspector may fine you). A single ticket (one metro ride or 75 minutes bus travel) costs 1,500 L but an all-day ticket with unlimited rides is a bargain at 6,000 L.

Rome's metro is not as useful as the ones in Milan and Naples, but it's worth carrying a metro map in case it offers a combination you need. If you happen to be at the Spanish Steps, for example, and you want to get to the Colosseum, then you'd head for the metro station off Via della Croce, take the Linea A train to Termini, change there to Linea B going south and get out at Colosseo. If you were at St Peters and you wanted to get to the Forum, you'd take bus number 64 and get out at Piazza Venezia.

In front of Termini station is a vast parking area for buses going to small towns throughout the Lazio region. The people in the information booths will write down instructions on how to reach your destination.

They may also have other advice. When I approached a booth to find out how to reach Ostia Antica, I asked the man if he spoke English and he replied: 'Sometimes, and this is one of my days'. He said Ostia was too hot to visit in the middle of the day, and did I have a second choice? I nominated Frascati, and he told me it contained a cafe serving the best ice cream in the world. Along with my transport instructions, he gave me a note for the manager of the Belvedere, telling him to give us his best ice cream. In the event, we didn't try the Belvedere, because we found a restaurant with a view (called Cacciani). If you get a chance to try the Belvedere, would you let me know how the ice cream is?

Footnote: There aren't many public toilets in Italy. If you get the urge while walking around, it's best to go into the nearest bar or cafe and head for the back, where the toilet usually is. The thing to ask for is *vee-chee* (WC) or *i gabinetti*, as in '*Per piacere, dove i gabinetti?*' ('Please, where are the toilets?').

PRACTICALITIES

96
the post office

You will usually encounter a long queue at a post office, because they serve as agencies for all manner of official business, they operate on bizarre rules which make simple activities like weighing a parcel take many minutes, and they close at 2 p.m. You don't have to buy stamps (*francobolli*) at a post office—newsagents or tobacco shops (marked with a giant T) will sell them. An airmail letter or postcard to Australia will need 1400 L worth of stamps (*mille quattrocento lire*).

Once posted, a letter will take up to a week to reach a destination within Italy, and two weeks to reach another country. For a higher price, you can have a letter sent *espresso*, which might reduce the local delivery time to two days and the international to eight. But it's better to send a fax—an understandably thriving industry in Italy these days.

Useful phrases:

How much to send this by airmail to Australia? *Quant'è l'affrancatura per Australia via aerea?*

I'd like some stamps, please. *Vorrei dei francobolli per favore.*

I would like an aerogramme. *Vorrei un'aerogramma.*

PRACTICALITIES

97
the phone system

*h*otels are expensive places to make international calls. Public phones are cheaper. If it's to someone who will accept the charges, dial 170 and ask the operator: '*Vorrei fare una chiamata a carico del destinario*' (vorray fah-reh oona key-uh-mah-tuh uh kureekoh del destinahreeyo), which means 'I'd like to make a reverse charges call'. In case the operator doesn't speak English, have your phrasebook or dictionary open at the page covering numbers. If you're calling someone who won't accept the charges, you should buy at least one phone card (*scheda telefonica*) worth 15,000 lire, from a newsstand or tobacconist, and insert it into the phone (after tearing off the corner). Then dial 00 followed by the country code and so on.

To make local calls from a public phone, you could use a phone card or some *gettoni* (jet-oh-nee)—metal tokens worth 200 lire each. The number for local information is 12 and for international information is 176. When answering, Italians say *pronto* (ready) instead of hello.

PRACTICALITIES

98
shopping

My own view is that shopping is a waste of good siesta time, but I know there are many people who see a visit to Italy as the chance to make some once-in-a-lifetime purchases. Italians are very good at making things, but they're aware of their reputation for quality, so there are no bargains anymore. Still, if you're from outside the European Union, you can get a refund on sales tax for items costing more than 300,000 lire in any one shop, as long as you don't mind the paperwork (get an invoice from the shop, have it stamped by Customs at the airport, send it to the shop within 90 days and they are supposed to send you the refund).

If you're happy to pay big bucks for a unique item you'd never find at home, here's an overview of the shopping options . . .

☆ **ANTIQUES**. The country is full of them, though most aren't for sale. In Rome, the key street for expensive old stuff is Via dei Coronari near Piazza Navona (for example Galleria Coronari at number 59). For old prints and artworks, wander along Via del Babuino

THE 100 THINGS . . .

near the Spanish Steps (Artimport is at 150).

☆ **BOOKS**. Italy has some odd English language bookshops which often contain volumes you'd never see in Australia, America or Britain. In Rome, try the Lion, 181 Via del Babuino; in Florence, BM Bookshop, 4R Borgo Ognissanti; in Milan, the American Bookstore at 16 Via Camperio.

☆ **CLOTHES**. It must be Milan (in January when the sales are on), particularly around Via Montenapoleone, but there are lower prices along Via Madonnina near the Brera Museum. A store with genuine discounts is Giuseppe Falzone at 5 Corso Cristoforo Colombo. In Rome, the fashion streets are all around the bottom of the Spanish Steps.

☆ **FLEA MARKET**. In Rome, head for Porta Portese in Trastevere, preferably on a Sunday morning.

☆ **FOOD**. In Milan, it must be Peck, the cathedral of cuisine, with several shops along Via Victor Hugo near the cathedral; in Bologna, Tamburini at 1 Via Caprare is a visual feast.

☆ **GLASS**. It must be Venice, but you should know that much Venetian glass is a) vulgar; and b) made in the Czech republic. To avoid these problems, try a factory called The Domus, 82 Fondamenta dei Vetrai, Murano; or Venini on Piazzetta Leoncini near St Mark's.

PRACTICALITIES

☆ **JEWELLERY**. In Rome, Bulgari's headquarters are at 10 Via Condotti; in Florence, the hot goldsmiths are Befani e Tai, 13R Via Vacchereccia; in Venice it's Missiaglia, 125 Piazza San Marco.

☆ **LEATHER**. Florence is said to have the greatest range, and there's original work at Beltrami Spa (1 Via del Panzini) and Bojola (25R Via dei Rondinelli). In Rome, try Alfieri at 2 Via del Corso, or Casagrande at 206 Via Cola di Rienzo; in Venice, try Marforio, Campo San Salvador, near St Mark's.

☆ **MASKS**. If you want to create your own *commedia dell'arte*, the best carnival masks in Venice come from Laboratorio Artigiano Maschere, Castello 6657, Barbaria delle Tole, near the Rialto bridge.

☆ **PAPER**. The most beautiful marbled paper and decorated stationery can be found in Florence at Giulio Giannini (37R Piazza Pitti) and Il Papiro (55R Via Cavour); in Venice, try Antica Legatoria Piazzesi, Santa Maria del Giglio, near St Mark's.

☆ **SHOES**. In Florence, Ferragamo's HQ is at 16R Via dei Tornabuoni.

☆ **SILKS**. Como (on Lake Como, north of Milan) is where it's all made, by worms descended from the ones brought back from China by Marco Polo in the 13th century. Try Ratti at 17 Via per Chernobbio.

PRACTICALITIES

99 guidebooks

*a*s I suggested in the introduction, this isn't really a guidebook. To get the most out of your travels, you should do more homework. Here are some paperbacks I try to carry with me whenever I visit ...

The Food of Italy, by Waverly Root (Vintage Books). Although written in 1971, before much of Italy's cooking traditions got lost in the tourist rush, it remains the essential analysis of the importance of eating in Italy's psychology.

Italy for the Gourmet Traveller, by Fred Plotkin (Kyle Cathie Ltd). Up to date advice on eating and drinking opportunities.

The green **Michelin**. Solemn but scrupulously detailed on the history of anywhere you're likely to visit.

Let's Go Italy (St Martin's Press). Hopeless on food advice (unless you want pizza), but a practical perspective on Italy now rather than Italy then.

PRACTICALITIES

Italy, by Dana Facaros and Michael Pauls (the Cadogan Guide). Irreverent and thoughtful, the English perspective is a relief after the American guides' obsession with bargain hunting and safe eating. It recommends trying the donkey stew in Mantua.

And the most elegantly written analysis of the national psyche is *The Italians* by Luigi Barzini (Hamish Hamilton). Published in 1964, it's still a stimulating insight.

PIONEERS

100
next

a pragmatic but humane government that stays in power till the year 2001. An efficient and honest public service. Most major crime bosses either dead or in prison. A booming economy that overtakes the economies of France and Britain, without inflation and without huge public debt.

Can this be Italy we're talking about? That's an optimistic vision of the next couple of years, but not an unrealistic one, given current patterns. The current period of stability is unprecedented in two centuries. Will the freedom to get on with talking, eating, creating beautiful things and preparing to win the 2002 World Cup be enough for Italians? How will they cope without the constant stimulation of crises and conspiracies?

Next year is the ideal time to watch how the people of the world's favourite country manage their latest triumph. I'll see you there.

acknowledgements

My largest load of gratitude goes to my friend Paolo Totaro, who undertook the burden of reading my work and whose thoughtful observations saved me from many embarrassments. Any remaining errors of fact or follies of judgement are because I failed to follow his advice. I'm grateful also for the insights of Lucio Galletto, Robert Gay, Mario Guelfi, Giampaolo Pertosi, Armando Percuoco, Beppi and Marc Polese, Paola and Mariella Totaro, Robert Veel and the Zuzza family, who have all given me a sense of Italians that no books or news reports could offer.

Cathy Wilcox more than doubled the book's value with her cartoons; Virginia Lloyd polished my prose and punctuation; Beth McKinley and Lloyd Foye indulged my obsession with getting a modern woman onto the cover; and Nikki Christer took the gamble that there were still some things Australians wanted to know about Italy.

These books were helpful in my research: *The New Italians*, by Charles Richards (Penguin); *Italy The Unfinished Revolution*, by Matt Frei (Mandarin); *Culture Shock! Italy* by Raymond Flower and Alessandro Falassi (Kuperard); *Great*

THE 100 THINGS ...

Italian Films by Jerry Vermilye (Citadel Press); *Getting It Right in Italy*, by William Ward (Bloomsbury); *Midnight in Sicily*, by Peter Robb (Duffy & Snellgrove); *An Italian Education*, by Tim Parks (Minerva); *Chambers Biographical Dictionary* (Chambers); *Frommer's 98 Italy*, by Darwin Porter and Danforth Prince (Macmillan); *Eyewitness Guide Italy* (Dorling Kindersley); and the guides listed in chapter 99.

Two Internet sites gave me daily data fixes while I was writing this book. The site created by the news service AGI (Agencia Giornalistica Italia) includes a daily summary in English of the main happenings in Italian politics, business, sport and society. Its address is www.agenziaitalia.it. And the Italian embassy in Washington has an elaborate site with advice on what to see and do in Italy, as well as links to data from the CIA, the US State Department, and the Italian bureau of statistics. Its address is www.italyemb.org.

index

Abortion, 83, 116,
Abruzzo, 194,
Adriatic Sea, 1
Agnelli, 108, 109, 115
Agrigento, 209,
Airmail, 181, 247
Airports, 236
Alba, 190
Alberobello, 229
Alessi, 87
Allen, Woody, 164
Alphabet, 30
Ancona, 193
Andreotti, Giulio, 7, 11, 40
Animals, 123
Antipasto, 51
Antiques, 249
Antonioni, 153
Appenine Mountains, 1
Archimedes, 179
Architecture, 168
ARCI-Gay, 118
Ariosto, 97
Armani, 12, 90
Arno River, 92
Art, 165
Artificial insemination, 181
Asinelli Tower, Bologna, 18, 226
Assisi, 67, 202, 203, 230,
Augustus, 93
Azzurri, 78

Baggio, Roberto, 7, 79, 81
Bari, 195
Baroque, 167, 169,
Barzini, Luigi, i, 253
Basilicata, 195
Basketball, 81
Bella figura, 12, 114
Bellini, 167
Benedetti, Carlo, 115
Benetton, 90
Benigni, Roberto, 154, 186
Bergamo, 186
Berio, 178
Berlusconi, Silvio, 5, 49, 79, 109, 115, 149, 150
Bernini, 171
Bertolucci, 157
Biagi, Enzo, 148
Bicycling, 82
Boccacio, 32, 160
Bologna, 7, 18, 54, 55, 66, 79, 118, 179, 185, 192, 226
Bongiorno, Mike, 151
Books, 159, 163, 250, 252
Borgias, 23, 180,
Borromeo Islands, 213
Borromini, 171
Bossi, Umberto, 6
Breakfast, 51
Brothels, 84
Brunelleschi, 170
Brusati, Franco, 157, 158

Brutta figura, 13
Buon Ricordo restaurants, 62
Buses, 243, 245
Business, 107

Caesar, Julius, 21, 93, 159
Cagliari, 196
Calabria, 195
Calvino, 161
Camonica Valley, 165
Camorra, 133
Campania, 68, 194
Campanilismo, 187
Campobasso, 194
Cancer, 145
Canova, 167
Cappuccino, 73, 103,
Capri, 16, 212
Carabinieri, 135,
Caravaggio, 167
Carducci, 160
Carraci, 167
Carrara, 16, 199
Cars, 3, 85, 242
Catacombs, 125
Catanzaro, 195
Catholic Church, 3, 14, 25, 44, 83, 97, 120
Cats, 123
Cavour, 100
Cecchi Gori, Vittorio, 154
Chianti, 71
Chiesa, Mario, 45
Children, 139

THE 100 THINGS ...

Christian Democrats, 6, 7, 11, 46, 48, 107, 126, 134, 150
Christianity, 22, 125, 166
Cicciolina, 27
Cimabue, 166,
Cinecittà, 153, 154
Clare, Saint, 202,
Clean Hands investigation, 5, 45, 49, 143, 110,
Clothes, 12, 250
Coffee, 73
Collodi, 161
Colombo, Cristoforo, 24,
Colosseum, 245
Commedia dell'arte, 185
Communists, 7, 48, 50, 110, 150
Como, 171
Condoms, 83, 181,
Constantine, 93, 125, 128
Constantinople (Byzantium), 93, 94, 128
Convento dei Cappuccini, Palermo, 17
Corelli, 173,
Corleone, Sicily, 134
Corriere della Sera, 108, 148
Corruption, 45
Cosa Nostra, 6, 134
Craxi, Bettino, 6, 46
Cremation, 145, 181
Crime, 132-137

d'Annunzio, 160
Danieli Hotel, Venice, 238
Dante, 19, 22, 32, 159, 163, 199
De Chirico, 167
De Sica, Vittorio, 153, 155, 156
Death, 145
Del Piero, Alessandro, 79
Design, 87
Di Pietro, Antonio, 5, 45, 46
Dialects, 32
Dietrologia, 10, 11, 136
Disasters, 230
Divine Comedy, 19, 22, 163, 199,
Divorce, 116, 120
Doctors, 143
Dogs, 123
Dolce Vita, 26, 104
Donatello, 167
Donizetti, 177
Driving, 85, 242
Drug addicts, 132

Earthquakes, 230
Eco, Umberto, 16, 26, 161
Economy, 105
Education, 141
Egadi Islands, 213
Elba, 212
Emilia-Romagna, 66, 192
Erice, 209
Espresso, 149, 182
Este family, 97
Etna, 17, 210
Etruscans, 92, 165, 173, 202

European Union, 55, 75, 105
Eva Tremila magazine, 19, 149
Exams, 141

Falcone, Giovanni, 134
Family, 14
Fantiscritti quarry, 16
Fax machine, 182, 247
Fellini, 26, 153, 155, 156
Fermi, 179
Ferrara, 97
Ferrari, 82, 85
Fiat, 46, 79, 85, 108, 115, 134
Films, 155
Fini, Gianfranco, 50
Florence, 22, 23, 95, 96, 97, 166, 169, 170, 192, 197, 223, 228
Fo, Dario, 162
Forza Italia, 5, 109, 113, 49, 50
Francis, Saint, 166, 202, 234,
Frascati, 62, 245
Friuli, 191
Funerals, 145
Futurism, 167

Gabrieli, 173
Galileo, 24, 179, 180
Garibaldi, 25, 100
Gays, 118
Gelli, Licio, 7
Genoa, 24, 25, 42, 54, 55, 191, 228
Gestures, 37

INDEX

Ghibellines, 95
Giorgione, 167
Giotto, 166
Giugiaro, Giorgio, 85
Giurgola, 171
Glass, 250
Goldoni, 160, 186
Government, 42, 48, 107
Graffiti, 39
Gramsci, 161
Grappa, 72
Greens, 49
Guardia di Finanza, 74, 135
Gubbio, 67, 203
Gucci, 89, 90
Guelphs, 95
Guidebooks, 252
Gypsies, 132, 146

Hadrian, 169
Hannibal, 92, 206
Hazan, Marcella, 27
Health, 143
Heart disease, 3, 145
Holidays, 234
Homes, 121
Homosexuals, 118
Honours, 114
Hospitals, 143
Hotels, 238 (and under their towns)
Housework, 117
Hypochondria, 143

Immigration, 146
IRI, 107
Ischia, 212

Jail, 137
Jesus, 125,166

Jewellery, 251
Jews, 127
John Paul II, 131
Jupiter, 124
Justinian, 94
Juventus soccer team, 18, 79

Kidnapping, 8
Kings of Italy, 25, 42, 100, 101
Knights of Malta, 215

Lampedusa, 161
Landini, 173
Last Supper, 16, 217
Latin, 32, 163
Lazio, 68, 193
Leather, 251
Lecce, 229
Leonardo Da Vinci, 16, 23, 97, 166, 179
Leoncavallo, 177
Leopardi, 160
Liguria, 65, 191
Limoncello, 74
Lipari Islands, 69, 213
Lollobridgida, Gina, 153
Lombards, 94
Lombardy, 64, 190
Loren, Sophia, 18, 26
Lucca, 17, 197,
Lunch, 51

Macchiavelli, 23, 160
Mafia, 6, 7, 11, 12, 133, 138
Magazines, 149

Magistrates, 137
Manzoni, 160
Marche, 67, 193
Marinetti, 161, 167
Marriage, 120
Mascagni, 177
Masks, 251
Mastroianni, Marcello, 18 153, 154, 156
Mazzini, Giuseppe, 99
Medici family, 22, 97
Memphis, 87
Metro, 245
Michelangelo, 16, 22, 24, 166, 170,199
Michelin guide, 59, 252
Middle Ages, 94
Milan, 13, 16, 18, 19, 23, 26, 45, 51, 62, 87, 89, 95, 96, 97, 109, 118, 186, 190, 217, 237
Military service, 139
Modigliani, 167
Molise, 5, 194,
Monreale, 209
Monte Solaro, Capri, 16
Monteverdi, 176
Moravia, 161
Moro, Aldo, 6
Moroccans, 146
Morricone, Ennio, 174
Mosaics, 166
Mothers, 15
Movies, 155
Murder, 132

THE 100 THINGS . . .

Murdoch, Rupert, 110
Music, 173
Mussolini, 26, 32, 54, 101, 107, 126, 134, 137, 153,

Name of the Rose, 16, 26, 161
Naples, 16, 18, 25, 33, 56, 57, 68, 96, 97, 100, 133, 140, 174, 176, 186, 194, 224, 229
Napoleon, 98, 99, 217
National Alliance, 49, 50, 113
Ndrangheta, 133
Nepotism, 15
Nero, 21, 93, 125
Nervi, 171
Newspapers, 148
Norcia, 206
Northern League, 6, 49, 110, 113

Olive Tree coalition, 5, 6, 49
Olivetti, 8, 46, 115
Opera, 178
Orvieto, 204
Ostia Antica, 246
Over-rated places, 228
Ovid, 159

P2 Lodge, 7
Padua, 63, 181
Paganini, 174
Palermo, 17, 196, 208

Palestrina, 173
Palio, 192
Palladio, 170
Parliament, 43
Passegiata, 77
Pasta, 51-53, 86, 103, 183
Pavarotti, 26, 178
PDS (Party of the Left), 48, 113
Peck, 217, 250
Perugia, 193
Pesto, 55
Petrarch, 32, 97, 160
Petronius, 159
Phones, 248
Piacentini, 171
Piano, Renzo, 172
Piazza Armerina, 210
Piemonte, 64, 189
Pininfarina, Sergio, 85
Pinocchio 39, 161
Pirandello, 161
Pisa, 24, 201, 236
Pizza, 56
Po River, 1
Polenta, 51, 181
Police, 135
Politics, 42-50
Polo, Marco, 53
Pompeii, 16, 39, 56
Ponziane Islands, 214
Pop music, 174
Popes, 11, 24, 125, 128-131
Population, 3
Porcini mushrooms, 58
Portofino, 228
Post office, 247
Potenza, 195

President, 42
Prodi, Romano, 5, 30, 49, 50, 107
Pronunciation, 28
Prostitution, 84
Provinces, 43
Public servants, 9, 112
Puccini, 178, 198
Puglia, 68, 195

RAI, 107, 150
Raphael, 166
Ravenna, 94, 166
Red Brigades, 7, 11
Reformation, 130
Regions, 43, 63, 189
Religion, 3, 124-131
Renaissance, 96, 129
Repubblica, 148
Restaurants, 58, 62 (and under their towns)
Riina, Salvatore, 6, 134
Risorgimento, 99
Risotto, 51
Robbery, 132
Rococo, 167, 169
Romans, 92, 165, 168
Rome, 16, 18, 21, 45, 63, 68, 92, 94, 123, 128, 169, 193, 219, 237, 245
Romulus and Remus, 21, 92
Rossini, 177

San Gimignano, 228
San Marino, 215
Sardegna, 69, 196

260

INDEX

Satan, 164
Savanarola, 54
Scalfaro, Oscar, 42
Scarlatti, 174, 176
Schools, 141
Science, 179
Secret services, 136
Segesta, 209
Seidler, Harry, 171
Seismograph, 183
Senate, 43
Sex, 83
Sforza family, 23, 97
Shoes, 251
Shopping, 249
Sicily, 25, 11, 17, 33, 51, 69, 94, 102, 134, 196, 208, 237
Siena, 95
Siesta, 75
Signs, 39
Silks, 251
Skiing, 82, 189
Soccer, 7, 18, 78
Socialist Party, 6, 45, 46, 49, 150
Sordi, Alberto, 154
Sorrento, 228
Spanish Steps, 245, 250
St Peters, 170
Stampa, 108, 148
Status, 114,
Suicide, 145
Sutherland, Joan, 26
Swimming, 82
Syracuse, 179, 211

Tacitus, 159,
Tangentopoli, 45,
Taormina, 208, 210, 228
Tasso, 97, 160
Taviani Brothers, 158
Telephone, 183
Television, 18, 150
Terragni, 171
Thomas Cook timetable, 241
Three Tenors, 26
Tiber (Tevere) River, 92
Tiberius, 93
Tiepolo, 167
Tindari, 228
Titian, 97, 167
Tivoli, 170
Tognazzi, Ugo, 154
Torcolato wine, 71
Torgiano, 67, 206
Toricelli, 179
Torre di Giano wine, 72
Toto, 154
Trains, 19, 241
Transsexuals, 84
Trasimeno, 206
Trentino-Alto Adige, 66, 190
Trento, 190
Trevi fountain, Rome, 20, 169
Trieste, 191
Truffles, 205
Turin, 26, 17, 189, 228
Tuscany, 17, 32, 33, 66, 192, 197
Tyrrhenian Sea, 1

Ubaldo, Saint, 203

Umbria, 67, 193, 202
Unions, 44
Universities, 142
Valentino, 91

Valle d'Aosta, 64, 189
Vatican, 101, 118, 126, 129, 215
Veneto, 65, 191
Venice, 16,19, 27, 59, 65, 95, 96, 107, 167, 173, 174, 186, 191, 221, 236
Verdi, 25, 177
Versace, 19, 89, 91
Vicenza, 170
Vieri, Christian, 79
Virgil, 159
Visconti, 153, 155
Vivaldi, 25, 174
Volta, 179

Weather, 184, 232
Welles, Orson, 180
Wertmuller, Lina, 157
Wine, 70
Women, 116
Work, 112, 116
World Cup, 7, 26, 79, 254

Yesterday, Today and Tomorrow, 18, 157

Zegna, 91
Zoos, 123